SECURING TOMORROW TODAY:

a path to quality education

Raymond A. Mensan

© **Raymond A. Mensah 2021**

All rights reserved

All rights reserved by author. No part of this publication may be reproduced, stored in a retrieval system or transmitted in any form or by any means, electronic, mechanical, photocopying, recording or otherwise, without the prior permission of the author.

Although every precaution has been taken to verify the accuracy of the information contained herein, the author and publisher assume no responsibility for any errors or omissions. No liability is assumed for damages that may result from the use of information contained within.

First Published in November 2021

ISBN: 978-93-5472-207-3

Price: INR 200/-

BLUEROSE PUBLISHERS
www.bluerosepublishers.com
info@bluerosepublishers.com
+91 8882 898 898

Cover Design:
Geetika

Typographic Design:
Namrata Saini

Distributed by: BlueRose, Amazon, Flipkart, Shopclues

Contents

Introduction 1

Part I Education 5
   The Beginning Of Quality Education 8

Part II The Launch Pads For Apex Learning 27
   Language 28
   Mathematics 32
   A Good Dose Of Adventure 36

Part III The Requirements For Academic Excellence . 47
   A Reading Culture 48
   Belief In Self 55
   The Quality Of Being Observant 59
   Independent Thinking Skills 63
   Team Spirit 68
   Proper Understanding Of Time 73

Part IV Pillars Of Quality Learning 80
   Self-Discovery 82
   Sound Values 95
   Self-Discipline 97
   Honesty 103
   Planning And Decision Making Skills 108

Part V Distractors **115**
   Sex And Amorous Feeling..116
   The Lure Of Money 123

Part VI   The Essence Of Education **127**
   The Link Between Education And Examinations 129
   Patriotism 142

Glossary **151**

Bibliography **163**

INTRODUCTION

Life on earth has always been full of needs in one way or the other. As a result, there has also been a constant need to be armed with certain skills to meet such needs or demands. Many of these demands do not only recur; they also come in different forms. This requires that we, as humans, be prepared to the best of our abilities if we must survive or develop; hence, our in-built quest for education. Therefore, education is as old as life on Earth.

It is said that the Europeans brought us education. But before their arrival, our forebears warred, farmed, and traded. They did many things to sustain themselves and make life as good as they could and wanted. The question is where did they get the skills to do what they did? Obviously, there learnt them. They may not have gone to classrooms to be taught, but they got themselves the skills they needed.

It is, therefore, not out of place to say that they were educated. Education can simply be defined as the process of acquiring knowledge, skills and values to sustain, or enhance life. Many of our forefathers did not attend any school, yet they got some form of education. Thus, it is obvious that schooling and education are two different things. Whereas the school is an invention, education is not. Also, there is an end to schooling, but education never ends. Education only ends at old age when people don't have the capacity anymore to learn the lessons that life teaches, or when people, full of life, decide to live like the aged.

Since it is understood that education is a product of schooling, schooling then can be thought of as a formal way of getting an education. Therefore, it is possible to go to school and not get the education it offers. Three things happen to anyone who goes to school: one, they may be uneducated; two, they may be mis-educated; and three, they may be educated. What becomes of any student in school depends on their own goals and what they do with their time there. Actually, the prestige or name of the school does not really matter.

Unlike the education our forefathers had, schools are aimed to offer superior education. In fact, this kind of education, to a large extent, accounts for the transformation the world has seen. Wherever schools have been, life has been better. The school, by its nature and what it offers, is the best place to go if people want to see the demonstration of discipline and refined human conduct.

However, for some reason, schools have not done much for the African continent, as we are left behind in so many areas in terms of human progress and attitudinal refinement. If schools are not able to yield the needed result, then it means something is wrong somewhere. And obviously, things in our country are not going the way they are supposed to go. There is the need to take a critical look at the situation and initiate steps to remedy it. The picture is not a pleasant one, and that is why you are herein called to duty. The truth is that your peers in some parts of the world are far ahead of you. And the gap does not just appear hopelessly wide - it keeps widening. It is indeed a worrying situation that can give you sleepless nights if you choose to be bothered. And it must bother you because the prevalence of such a situation is not in the interest of anyone.

The global community is a tough and competitive one. Signs of weaknesses are quickly and easily exploited by other competitors, so it is not advisable to show any. In competitions, the mistakes and weaknesses of opponents are always exploited, and they are to be.

Also, human slavery will never end by any means apart from quality education. Anybody who has received or is receiving an education that is better than what you have, or what you are giving yourself, is your potential master or mistress. The longer it takes to get quality education, the longer it will be to remain in slavery as individuals and as a country.

You may say, 'Ah, wait a minute, but we are independent!' We may be independent as a country, but individual slavery prevails. If your life depends heavily on someone, you are likely to be held a slave to that person. With poor education, apart from being a slave to external forces, you can also be enslaved by your own people who are more knowledgeable than you.

Therefore, the pursuit of your independence must be paramount, and the gap between you and your foreign counterparts must be narrowed to give the hope of an even-playing field. Additionally, the things that widen this gap make life in our part of the world one of endurance instead of enjoyment. And this, in itself, is a huge trap. This is how it works: since everybody wants to be free, naturally, our of these subjects should I study? Two, why should I study it? And three, how can the program I am choosing prepare me adequately to do what I love?

There should be a fair idea of what these programs are about and what they offer students so that the questions asked could be answered well. So at the end of the day, it is assumed that any student doing a particular program has certain things they are passionate about and that by offering that program, they will be equipped with the required knowledge and skills to do what they so much desire.

Unfortunately, there are many instances where the only reason some students have had to pursue a particular program is the kind of grade they had. When students get excellent grades, they are to be given General Science; good grades, General Arts and Business; and poor grades, Visual Arts and Home Economics. On some occasions, others offer certain programs because their parents want them to do such. Some parents may get it right by helping choose a program of study for the ward, having identified the ward's interest or passion. But on many occasions, that is not the case.

The danger of this is that it brings the student nowhere near quality education. This is because the student may be pursuing what they do not have any passion for. The best way, in such circumstances, is for the parents and ward to come to an agreement. The assistance of the parents is needed to guide the ward and not to impose a program on them. Getting a fair understanding of the programs offered at the senior high school should help students settle on the right programs.

BUSINESS STUDIES

There is the business aspect of almost every area of individual and national lives. Even non-profit organizations have their business sides. Among the subjects studied are management, accounting and economics. All things that have to do with the production of goods and services concern business. Individual homes and families need some level of business skills to improve upon themselves. Even countries and organizations require business skills to grow. Without business skills, schools, hospitals, organizations and countries will be crushed. Our country has some great business men and women. But on the international front, our businesses are not very strong.

Someone with passion for business will pursue the subject to set up businesses that would compete with other international organizations. At the age of seven, Warren E. Buffett was inspired by *Thousand Ways to Make $1000*, a book he borrowed from a public library. The very fact that he borrowed a book like that to read is enough proof that he had interest in making money. With guidance from his parents, he schooled and pursued business programs. Now he is one of the most established entrepreneurs and business men in the world. In fact, as a teenager, he owned not one, but several businesses.

The business world is very vast. And with passion for business, there will, by all means, be a place you can fulfil it. Knowledge in business will not only keep business outfits functional, but also make them better. Studying business equips people for the dynamically developing corporate world. With business studies, people can either set up their own businesses or work for others. It is such a picture and like the experience of Warren that inspires students to decide to spend their lives studying business to take care of their individual aspirations and the world's business needs.

VISUAL ARTS

What entertainment does for society is common knowledge. Just take a second and imagine a world without music and movies. People are normally heard saying they like nice things. Some kinds of phones and gadgets are so attractive that people are tempted to buy them without caring much about their functions. Normally, when people want to buy clothes, they take the time to search through and then settle on what might look good on them.

It is said that without visual art, the whole world will only be black and white. What is beautiful is beautiful and does not only work on the eye, but the soul as well. From the design of the houses we live in to the office complexes, bicycles to cars, aeroplanes to submarines, watches and jewellery; just name them—any man-made thing that is attractive has the touch of visual artists.

There are many ways of communicating. And one of the best ways is through paintings or pictures. A visual artist can say things in one painting that would take a writer bundle of plain sheets to write; and the speaker, days to say. This should give a strong impression of the visual artist: such cannot be a dull person! Creativity and powerful imagination are the hallmarks of a visual artist. The erroneous impression that visual art is a program for students who are not academically sharp is regrettable and must be a thing of the past. It is not only for boys. It is not for students who are not serious in school. It takes special minds to put what is not seen on paper. It takes special minds to make the world beautiful. The desire for nice things, to communicate special information, and the passion to make the world beautiful is what inspires students to pursue visual arts as a program. Until we move to a cashless era, we will continue to use hard currencies. Has it occurred to you that someone designed our currency? We take a Cedi note, appreciate the security signs and general design, and pass the comment, 'it is very nice'. What people fail to realize is that they are enjoying the skill of a hard-working Ghanaian visual artist.

Visual art is not only about painting; performing arts, textile arts and conceptual arts all involve aspects of visual artistry. There is a general cry that the country's movie industry lacks quality. The solution to many of the problems in the movie industry lies in the hands of visual artists. The opportunities in visual artistry are numerous. The internet and online businesses even make the opportunities for visual arts limitless.

It was in this field that Walt Disney found his success. All the cartoons that we watch are foreign and in foreign languages. Visual artists can produce quality African cartoons in African languages and in African settings – ones that can also be enjoyed by foreigners even as we enjoy theirs. We should see the Ghanaian Walt Disney in no time.

GENERAL ART

This is also another area of science. Under this area, the science of human behaviour and learning is studied. Individuals are unique and will remain unique. This uniqueness makes people do things differently. In a society of various individuals, different character and behavioural traits will manifest. The ignorance and misunderstanding of this individual uniqueness create a lot of problems in families and society.

To address these challenges, it is important to know what makes individuals unique and why it is so. Lack of answers to these questions accounts for the disputes and other forms of conflict in families and society. When people live in peace, they can combine their energies and resources for their common good. Countries can develop well when this aspect of the human side is developed. But where can knowledge and skills be obtained to do this?

Additionally, there must be the correct use of language for the good of society. Here, language is used in drama and other literary works to entertain and educate society. A misuse or under-use of language is detrimental to society. This calls for a better understanding and development of language.

The danger of language is that its neglect is the neglect of life. Language affords the opportunity to explore human nature. And the understanding of human nature can lead to the invention of good and practical systems of governance to enhance lives. For example, the Americans invented democracy as a better substitute for autocracy and monarchy. If we think democracy does not produce the required results, we can invent one that would suit us. But the question is if we indeed need a better system that would suit us, who would invent that for us?

Also, if something can be made anew, the old version must be understood. This means there can be no thought of a better future if the past is not known. The forgotten past makes the future illusive. To this end, available evidence must be used to trace the past. This is the work of history. How many museums do we have, and who cares about keeping the relics of our past?

In the United States, for example, the house of Abraham Lincoln, who died on 15 April 1865, is still there. Some of the furniture in his room, including the bed on which he slept, are still there for the younger generation and tourists to see. In sum, there must be better leadership and followership, an understanding among people in homes and institutions, knowledge of history, law and etc. A student with a strong urge to help the country and world in any of the above instances pursues the general art program for equipment.

HOME ECONOMICS

The word *home* in the name of the program should interest any curious mind. The life of society begins at home, so what goes wrong with the home goes wrong with the society. Therefore, any service rendered to the home is one to society, and vice-versa.

Over here, too, there are some misconceptions. One, this program is normally reserved for girls and so it is hardly run in boys schools. Because of this, boys who opt for this program in co-ed schools normally get ridiculed by their peers. And two, it is normally reserved for those who do not perform well in the Basic Education Certificate Examination (BECE).

The truth is that the food people eat makes them what they are. When people eat well, they live well. Many of the diseases and sicknesses in society today can be traced to poor eating; perhaps, due to lack of food science. This is the field where the area of food science can be learnt. So when people shy away from it for fear of what will be said about them, then we are left to eat whatever we find, and however we are able to make them.

But the country needs a strong and healthy workforce for good productivity. We all wish to stay healthy, but good health depends heavily on our diet. Some people leave the house for work very early and what to eat in the day becomes a problem. If many of the people who sell on our streets have basic knowledge of food science, what people, who are out of their homes, will need to eat will no longer be a problem.

Interestingly, home economics is not only about food since the home is not just about food. Special skills are needed to maintain a home. Health, safety and happiness are some of the needs at home, and this program equips people with these skills. People need good clothing and footwear not only to protect them, but to make them confident. The issue of people's personal wellness must also be taken care of. If anyone has passion to serve the world in any of the above areas, how can that be done - through the pursuit of home economics, of course? And, obviously, these cannot be done by girls alone. As can be said of the other areas, the field of home economics also presents limitless opportunities.

SCIENCE

The only thing that is unique about the field of science is that it is very broad. Generally, there are the biological and physical sciences. The physical sciences do not study living things. They include areas such as the Earth sciences, physics, chemistry and astronomy. The biological sciences, on the other hand, as the name implies, study living things or life. Some of the areas under this are botany, zoology and microbiology.

There are many precious minerals in the rocks to mine. The plants and trees in the forest are not only to be preserved; they have medicinal properties to be tapped. The rivers and winds have energies to be trapped for human consumption. The animals, apart from serving as food, have several features and properties to be harnessed. There are the oceans and space to explore, and there are roads, bridges, buildings and machines to make. In fact, the list seems endless. What make up the human body must be known and understood so that they can be fixed, should problems occur. Apart from these, there are many inventions that can be made to make life easier and better.

Science affords humans the opportunity to think correctly and analytically. When humans were not given to correct and analytical thinking, we had what was called the Dark Ages. The Dark Ages of mankind were simply ages where scientific knowledge was limited. There were many happenings humans attributed to Gods that were just natural occurrences. For example, earlier, in the history of man, lightning was believed to be an act of God. And if an act was an act of God, who would dare investigate it? As a result, buildings were destroyed and lives lost when lightning struck and set buildings ablaze. It is even recorded that people who wanted to escape the destruction of lightning sometimes hid in church buildings with the idea that God would not destroy his own house. Yet, they met the same fate.

But Benjamin Franklin, who was a scientist, defied the odds and thought differently. He studied and investigated lightning and discovered it was electricity. From this, he invented the lightning rod, which now protects buildings from lightening. You can imagine the number of buildings and lives that would still be destroyed by lightning if the world had not had a scientist like Benjamin Franklin. Like him and other scientists around the world, anyone who ventures into science wants to help answer some of life's toughest questions.

VOCATIONAL AND TECHNICAL TRAINING

Vocational and Technical Training is the life and need-based education that makes unskilled people good human resources for development. This kind of education is so vital that without it, society and nations grind to a halt. The essence of vocational and technical education is to provide knowledge and skills needed for agriculture, industry, commerce and the economy; to give an introduction to professional studies in engineering and other technologies, and to produce craftsmen and women, technicians and other skilled personnel who would establish their own businesses and be self-reliant.

One of the differences between this area and science is that a science student learns at the laboratory while a technical student learns at the workshop. Aside from this, the two are practical fields, so it does not require much writing. It is concerned primarily with knowledge and its application.

Like any other field of study, those who decide to go into vocational and technical training must begin with intelligent questions. They must be driven to that field by a particular passion for something. The situation where many students have had to go to Vocational and Technical schools because they did not do well in their BECE, or WASSCE should also be discouraged. Enrolling into a vocational and technical school is not about whether one passes their exams or not, but rather about whether they understand why they want to go to a vocational and technical school. It is about the individual's urgent need for a certain skill set to meet certain demands.

Our mining, oil and gas, and manufacturing industries are full of expatriates (foreign nationals) who are paid huge sums of money in foreign currencies that, at the end of the day, contribute to weakening our local currency, the Cedi. The country may have no option but to heavily rely on these expatriates because, on many occasions, they have the needed skills to get the work done. In the situation where we do have local technicians, they are not enough. With the vocational and technical schools, we can have enough people trained for our oil and gas, mining, and manufacturing industries.

Buildings require builders, and machines require manufacturers and operators. Every industrial setup works with machines in one way or the other. Nowadays, many of these machines are operated by robots, but a lot are still operated by humans. So the human factor is and will always be very important. Even in the car manufacturing industries, where robots do many of the work, humans are a necessity.

One of the reasons some countries are more developed than others is that they have a skilled workforce while the others do not. In the ancient times, the most prosperous kingdoms were those that had a lot of artisans. Those artisans made for them all the items they needed for their everyday use, for example, their weapons of war, cooking pots, boats, baskets, houses, etc. Artisans and technicians are needed today as they were needed in the past; perhaps more than before. This is why vocational and technical training is needed.

SPORTS

This is another important area of education. It is part of the activities in all schools in the country. But because it is not offered as an area of study, it is not given the needed attention. It is worth noting that sports are one of the best areas of employment in the world and offer one of the best paid career opportunities. Many of you are aware of the salaries some players are paid for just a week. There are numerous examples of people whose lives have been transformed by sports.

But there is more to sports than the money. Sports do not only benefit the players and athletes but the spectators as well. Spectators love to watch their favourite players and athletes in competitions. Some are ready to pay any amount of money to watch their stars in action. Furthermore, the health benefits of sports are many. For the players and athletes themselves, sports keep them fit and strong. For students, sports help with proper brain functioning and mental development.

The area of sports must be taken as seriously as any other area of student life. All over the world, basic sports are combined with academic work. This means that students have more time to learn and practice their sports as they do their academic studies as well. In this case, it is expected, on the part of the student, to give equal attention to both areas. Anytime there is an international tournament, it is realized that all the players of the European and American teams are from their various schools and universities.

But our case is always the opposite. We normally have about 1% of our teams as students while the rest are school dropouts. And even if they do complete any school at all, they normally do not have anything good to show for it. About 90 % of the players and athletes of sports teams in our various schools are habitual absentees. They normally do not go to school until it is time for sports. After the sports, they will not be seen again until the next sporting time.

If students in other countries combine sports with academics, our students can do the same here. Sports are not only for those who are not academically good. You can be a sports person and also pursue academics to any level you want. Ghanaian boxer and former world champion Isaac Dogboe is a very good example for all athletes. He boxed and schooled at the same time. He is a complete Ghanaian—the only difference is that he spent most of his time growing up in Europe. Ghana's 100m runner, Benjamin Azamati, is also a good example. At West Texas A&M University, in the United States, he lives his dream: running. He graduated from the University of Ghana, Legon.

To get more of Ghana's football legends Abedi Ayew Pele, Anthony Yeboah, and boxing legend Azumah Nelson, our students who are good at sports must be more passionate about it. They must desist from the acts of indiscipline and truancy. One of the things that destroy many sportsmen and women is indiscipline. If it is eschewed, a lot of success will be achieved in sports.

One of the challenges in this area is that the sporting calendar in our schools cannot produce world champions because it does not make enough room for sports training. Therefore, those with sporting talents must enrol in sporting academies, even if these academies can only be accessed outside the country. There are many students who can transform their lives and that of their families through sports. The areas of academic and vocational endeavours in sports are diverse.

The right questions need to be asked in order for students to pursue the right programs. Once there is enough evidence that you are in the correct field, what is left is to pursue it with all might and main. Many students have had to waste their precious time and years following what they did not have any interest for. It is time to start, and start right.

PART II

THE LAUNCH PADS FOR APEX LEARNING

There are factors to consider in anything worth doing. These factors are things without which that particular venture may fail. For example, when people want to put up any physical structure, one of the first considerations is the availability of land. If the issue of land becomes a challenge, there will be no way to start with the structure until it is resolved. In similar fashion, many things account for quality education on the part of the student. Among these, two are pre-requisites. How far a student may climb the academic ladder greatly depends on these two.

LANGUAGE

Language is to the mind more than light is to the eye.

William Gibson

It is hard to imagine what the brain can do without a language. Without language, the brain is almost useless. The brain, as part of its functions, interprets whatever signal it receives, whether sounds or symbols, and it dwells on the available language to do the interpretation. If it does not have enough language or words, the interpretation will be difficult.

What, then, becomes of the signal is that it would be treated in a manner it is not to be treated since it makes no sense. What this means is that the brain cannot do anything meaningful if it has no language to use. Luckily, there is no one without a language. This implies that every student has a language with which the brain can work. This is good news, but there is a challenge.

There are many languages in the country. Some are already lost and others are gradually slipping away. Some people are not even able to speak the language into which they were born. These are signs that the value or place of language is not really understood. And this is the challenge. There is a clear misunderstanding or underestimation of language because attention is not given to it. But for students to be ready for quality academic work there must be very good language proficiency.

A struggle with language is also one with thinking. And to struggle to think is to struggle to learn because learning is nothing but a thinking process. The good news is that every student is born into a family and society with a language. In fact, this language is the student's first and most important learning resource. Anything that interrupts proficiency in this first language interrupts the student's entire learning.

Therefore, to temper with this first language is to temper with the student's learning ability. To this end, every effort must be made to be good at that language, whether it is used at school or not. To master this language, it must be spoken regularly, and it must be heard a lot too. Unless there is a biological problem, people do not normally struggle to speak the language they are born into. As a result, they do not struggle with thinking and, by extension, their studies, if the learning takes place in their own language.

However, the situation for the Ghanaian student is different as academic work is carried out in English, and all books for academic work are written in the same. What this implies is that the Ghanaian student is expected to think in English. Whatever teachers teach and whatever is read from books must be processed in English. The task is that when faced with any academic challenge, the brain will depend on the amount of English words (vocabulary) the student has to interpret the information. The result is obvious for any student who struggles with the English language. The English language, in this regard, is one of the two most important launch pads for quality academic work. It is quite unfortunate, but we are left with no option so effort must be made to master it.

MASTERING THE ENGLISH LANGUAGE

It must be noted with keen interest that the English language lessons in the classroom alone cannot produce the proficiency needed for quality academic work. Language is for use, and the more it is used, the better it becomes. But the classroom cannot provide enough opportunity for the language to be used. With the understanding that language improves by use, speaking English regularly must be a duty. Therefore, it is not a good sign for students to be told to speak English before they do so. Students are not to only speak—they must also learn to listen to spoken English frequently as that helps a lot.

One of the best ways to learn a foreign language is to listen frequently to the speakers of that language speaking it. One can listen to local programs on our various media outlets in English and that will surely help in many ways. But, without question, the English proficiency of a learned Ghanaian cannot be better than the English proficiency of a learned British.

Therefore, one of the most effective ways to master the English language is to listen to programs and news on foreign media (radio and television). Quality movies in English can also help. While watching such movies, attention must be paid to the language structures and vocabulary the characters use. Additionally, all activities in school that offer an opportunity for English language practice must be taken advantage of. For example, drama, debates, club activities and poetry recitals are some of the things you must take interest in.

Finally, a reading culture must be developed. This culture will provide an exposure to a wide range of vocabulary and varied sentence structures. A combination of the things above will surely address a lot of the language deficiencies of students and help provide that spring-board for quality learning.

MATHEMATICS

But in my opinion, all things in nature occur mathematically.

Rene Descartes

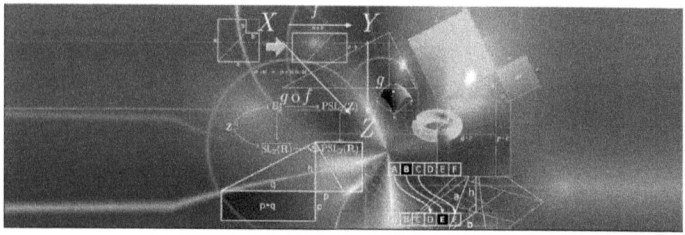

Mathematics goes hand in hand with language. It depends on the language available to develop. This means that a deficiency in language will negatively affect the learning of mathematics; a weak language is a hindrance to mathematics. Many students have very poor knowledge of mathematics. And this has led to a serious misconception of the subject. For instance, it is said that boys are inclined to do better in mathematics than girls. But this is false and dangerous as it builds a huge wall in the minds of many girls. This, at the end of the day, stops them from doing advanced studies in mathematics or venture into programs of studies that have components of mathematics. Even among boys, it is also believed that some are not cut for mathematics. This is also false.

What is true is that every single individual is expected to think clearly and correctly. Also, things must be done orderly and in the right manner if good results are to be expected. People should be able to notice changes in things around them. They should be able to create models of abstracts or things that are not concrete. Again, people should know why one thing leads to another, and why another thing does not lead to the other under similar or different circumstance. People should be able to identify parts from whole, etc.

The above are not expected from only a certain section or group of people. They are indeed expected from every single healthy person. And they are what mathematics is about. Mathematics is about logical and accurate thinking. It is about precision and brevity. For example, through algebra, a statement like ***the difference between four times a number and four is sixteen*** can be written as ***$4x-4=16$.*** This is not just clearer and easier than those written in words. With this equation, it is easy to find out what that particular number is. Everybody must think logically and correctly. Therefore, mathematics is about everything and for everybody. It is for everybody as language is for everybody. It is misinformation to think that mathematics is meant for some group of people.

There is no such thing as people who are born for mathematics and others who are not. Everybody can be good at mathematics. If anybody is skilled or very good at something, it means that person spends much time practising that particular thing. If someone is better at social studies than the English language, it means the person spends more time on social studies than they do on English. That is the secret.

The situation where many students fear mathematics is a very disturbing one because it weakens the foundation for serious learning that transforms society. It makes it difficult to produce a lot of students who can think through problems and come up with life-saving solutions.

This problem can be blamed on the ignorance of students and some teachers of the subject of mathematics. These teachers are largely responsible because of how they teach the subject. It has, for a long time, been handled poorly. This poor handling of mathematics presents a monstrous version of mathematics other than the genuine. Frankly, any light-hearted person will run away from a monster! And such teachers present nothing but a monster all the time. The real mathematics has an arresting beauty. It is about freedom, it is about creativity; it is about wired and risky ideas (thinking outside the box). It is hard to resist the temptation of mathematics. This is what happened to the Indian mathematical genius Srinivasa Ramanuja (the man who knew infinity). When he discovered what mathematics was, he was so in love with it that he did not have time for other subjects.

A sound understanding and good control over mathematics is needed for quality learning. As a result, every effort must be made to achieve a better understanding of it. A solid foundation of love for mathematics is needed to excel in visual arts, business, home economics, general arts, and technical studies. Nothing exercises the brain perhaps more than mathematics. To a large extent, it is the gym for the brain. As people need the gym to stay fit, mathematics is needed for the brain to stay fit—no two ways about that. Whenever you sit alone or in a class for mathematics, remember that you are at the mental gym for a mental workout—just enjoy it!

To do well in mathematics, a good knowledge of its history will help as this may get you fascinated about the origins of many of the mathematical symbols and concepts. Mathematics has a beginning. It does not help to try to know something without caring about how it all began. Nothing can be as reckless as that. Also, to be prepared for mathematics, students should be ready to accept the truth about mathematics and reject the falsehood. Further, students must spend quality time thinking about and learning mathematics. Students must concentrate on understanding concepts rather than memorizing formulae.

The good news is that it is never too late for any student to pick up in mathematics. Therefore, the one who is struggling with mathematics does not need to worry at all. For anyone in such condition, there are things about mathematics that are hidden from them. What must be done is first, to have the desire to learn the subject, and next, to get a good teacher who will help find what is hidden. This will lead to something like a scale falling from the eyes. They will be amazed to, for the first time, see the beautiful thing they have all the while been running away from. This state of mathematical awareness and a good command of the English language are the spring-boards to lunch Ghanaian students into new heights of intellectual inquiry and academic pursuit.

A GOOD DOSE OF ADVENTURE

Life is either a daring adventure or nothing.

Helen Keller

Life is a hunting expedition of a sort. Nothing comes on a silver platter, so we are always on a search for one thing or the other. We are always, in one way or the other, looking for something to satisfy a need. For example, someone going to the stadium to watch a football match has a need they want satisfied. Someone looking for a cup of water has a need they to satisfy.

But the whole hunting business is as an adventure and it takes the adventurous to embark on an adventure. Some of these hunters hunt in the night when vision is hugely constrained. Also, there are many terrible predators in the forest. So it takes boldness to be hunters.

Since life compares to hunting, being reasonably adventurous is key to success, especially as a student. There can be no solid foundation for learning without a sense of adventure. If your future, that of family, the country and the world at large will be shaped by the things you will do, then you must develop an adventurous spirit.

For example, just the mere sight of the sea for the very first time is dizzying. So what made explorers attempt to cross the oceans to distant lands? The ability to make the attempt not only to step into the sea but to sail across it is a good example of the trait of adventure. To dare possible dangers and do what you want to do is adventure.

It was adventure that took the first man to the moon. It was adventure that made the very first sailor. If Christopher Columbus was fearful, he would not have seen that land now called America. It was adventure that brought the first European to Africa and took the first African to Europe.

And truly, the adventurous is always ahead of the fearful. Abraham Maslow said, 'You will either step forward into growth, or you will step backward into safety.' There are many things students in advanced countries may attempt to do that our students may not venture towards at all. Since they are those who will lead their countries in the future, their countries have an advantage over ours. To close the gap, a daring spirit is needed—you must be adventurous.

People in search of knowledge must be prepared to go to horrific and unpleasant places. It takes audacity to be a diver, to be able to go to the sea bed or the floor of the sea where there are great whales and other predatory fishes. It is audacity that will enable our young men and women in the army to fly our fighter jets and planes with extraordinary skills and manoeuvres in the air. It takes adventure to do something you have not experienced, and to do what no one has done before.

Be daring and ready to climb the mountains and descend the valleys; ford the rivers and sail the seas; explore the sea beds and venture into space; explore the forest belts and ignore what is called the evil forest; enter into caves, and go everywhere you can to seek knowledge.

Adventure will help you overcome fear; it will build and increase self-confidence, and also equip you with the ability to face challenging times in your life. There are some activities that can help with adventure. Travelling and touring special sites can help. Biking and youth camping also help. But sadly, some of these things are quite remote in our setting.

But more importantly, you can read books and watch movies that are adventurous. In doing this, you need to be fascinated with the main characters in them. Try to associate with them. And explore what you would do if you were those characters.

In school, especially boarding houses, some students break bounds, and attempt many risky things, knowing very well that they could land in trouble. But they do them anyway. Obviously, such students are fearless and have a good deal of self-confidence.

However, this is not the kind of adventure in question for obvious reasons. Such people do not just waste their time, but their activities may also get them sacked from school, and this behaviour prepares them for delinquency, future struggles and hardships. In essence, it robs them of education and therefore, must be shunned. Practice what is beneficial.

GETTING THE CONCEPT OF LEARNING

Surface knowledge is the traditional memorization of facts and procedures. To acquire meaningful knowledge however, students must be able to perceive relationships and patterns to make sense of information. Students make sense of information by relating it to their unique past experiences and current environmental context and interactions. (Caine & Caine 1991)

What happens if students who are in school to learn do not know what learning is? The result is that they are likely to think they are learning when they are actually not learning at all. They leave the learning institutions and realize they know almost nothing. To avoid this waste of time and lives, it is necessary to have a fair knowledge of the concept of learning. It is important to know what learning is so that steps can be taken to find out how it can best be done.

This will help those who want to learn know that they are learning and also be able to find ways to learn better. For example, it is important to know why five plus five is ten, but five times five is twenty-five. Learning requires that you are not just able to remember that, but to understand what it means and why.

It has been wrongly believed that learning is the memory of facts and procedures. Actually, memory is part of learning, and perhaps, that may be why the impression is created that it is learning. But it is important to draw a line between what it means to learn and what it means to memorize.

It is also important to know that adolescent and adult learning is different from the learning of children or kids. Children receive information, but adolescents and adults receive education. When people are able to do things they could not have done because of the knowledge they have received, it means they have learned something (they have received education). But this normally cannot be done by kids. A kid may recite a poem excellently, yet may not know what the poem is about and what that poem does to the one who hears it. This is one reason a lot of them may be able to recite the alphabets from A-Z, yet not be able identify them in prints.

When people are able to memorize facts and procedures, they have not really learned anything yet. They have only had a success at memory. But memory just lies in the world of storage, which is completely different from learning. In fact, memory is only needed after learning has taken place. In learning, discoveries are made; learning is all about discoveries. To discover is to come across, find or be aware of something that exists which was never known existed. Learning is all about awareness.

The essence of the teaching activities in and outside the classrooms is to assist the understanding that would take students to this state of awareness. So in the teaching process, until a state of awareness of something is reached by the student, learning has not yet taken place. Teachers do not come to give pieces of information for students to store or remember. They come to help students discover facts for themselves.

When a discovery is made or awareness is reached, then it is taken note of, memorized or stored, to apply when needed. What is discovered does not even necessarily have to be memorized. They can be stored on a drive or written in a notebook for use anytime they are needed. It is only working knowledge that is memorized as this saves time and makes work less cumbersome.

This is why you do not necessarily need to have an excellent memory or photographic memory to be a good student. What makes an excellent or good student is the ability to understand and manipulate ideas, to realize differences and similarities, and to skilfully draw relationships between concepts and experiences.

It is obvious then, that memory is at the tail end of the learning spectrum. In other words, it completes the learning process so that until you learn, there is nothing to memorize.

Every text book that is picked up is a presentation of what people have discovered for themselves. They are not pieces of information to store and reproduce to meet examination requirements. The authors only attempt to help readers to also discover for themselves what they (the authors) have already discovered. The use of different sentence structures, words, diagrams pictures and many examples are to make it easy or less difficult for comprehension to take place.

You do not have anything again to do with the examples and illustrations they provide after you have understood the concepts. In fact, when you reach the state of understanding or awareness, you should be able to come up with your own examples and illustrations. If you struggle to come up with your own examples and illustrations, it means you have not yet understood it. Hence, you have not yet learned that particular thing.

REALIZING THE MARVEL OF THE BRAIN

The centre of the whole learning enterprise is the brain. It will be a great mistake to overlook it and seek to achieve meaningful education or produce quality human resources. It is believed that a minimum understanding of this special part of the human body may go a long way to help make the most of it.

Michio Kaku, an American scientist, said, 'The human brain has 100 billion neurons, each neuron connected to 10,000 other neurons. Sitting on your shoulders is the most complicated object in the known universe.' The complexity of the human brain perhaps attests to the complexity of issues it is meant to handle. The brain is specifically designed to solve almost all physical problems.

And, in fact, all things are possible. The things that are impossible are those that are thought to be impossible. Remember that almost all the things that have changed lives today were once thought to be impossible. If anything cannot be done now, it only means that it has not yet been discovered how it is done, that is all. And this is all that education is about: to know what is not yet known and to understand what is not yet understood.

The brain is meant to be trained and exercised. With enough training and right information, the brain can attend to almost all human challenges. It is made up of several billions of cells, and can do so many things that we are not yet aware of. Its mode of operation is fascinating. The brain, in training, is like a muscle; the more it gets exercised, the stronger it becomes. The moment you stop exercising, the muscles become weak and unable to perform simple body drills. Like the muscles, the more you give your brain hard and complex work, the better and much improved it becomes. You will have to give it the best training you can.

The brain works with pathways. You realize that normally you find it difficult or uncomfortable doing something for the first time. The reason is that your brain does not have any pathway for that thing since it is new. But as you keep practising and doing it, your brain eventually creates a pathway for it, and then it becomes easier for you to do that thing.

When you stop doing that particular thing for a very long time, the pathway gets 'erased', and you begin to struggle doing that thing again. In other to create very strong pathways, you need to practice a lot. The secret is that any student good at mathematics has a very strong pathway for mathematics, and any student good at English, social studies, visual arts, etc., has strong pathways for them.

Your brain is your greatest treasure, not your parents' wealth. This is why parents who love their children dearly do everything, even if they have to sell what they have, to give them the best training the brain can get. It is your storeroom, your bank account, wardrobe and everything. It is therefore not surprising that you came into this world naked, and with nothing. The fact is that everything you will need on earth is supposed to be worked out by your brain. It is protected by a pretty hard skull because it is your greatest asset and must not be played with.

Your brain is a great mine site that no one shares with you. You do not need any license or anyone's permission to exploit it. Whatever there is that your brain is capable of is your own. As mineral resources are exploited, so should the brain. Another way of making the most of your brain is to be daring in your thinking.

You do not have to be afraid to entertain new ideas. Do not be afraid to investigate anything that questions what you already know. This investigation is important because it is possible what you think is right is actually wrong, and what you think is wrong is actually right. You need to fully exploit your brain for your own good, and the good of the country. Societies are transformed primarily with brains. The availability of natural resources is just an advantage.

It is important to do body exercises since they contribute to the development of the brain. Playing football, volley ball, swimming, jogging, etc. can help the brain in many ways. There is virtually no limit to what a sharp brain can do.

Since it is your greatest weapon, it will pay to have it in the best of shapes. Search the net and look for some brain games or invent one for yourself. When you are tired after a hard day's work, play some brain games to relax. Follow Jim Kwick, Dominic O'Brien and other brain coaches on YouTube to learn more about how you can make the most of your brain.

Concerning the stages of life, you are at the preparatory stage—the stage for the acquisition of knowledge of the fundamentals of life. Therefore, what must engage you now is the search for knowledge. This means that your place of employment is the school, and your work is the sharpening of your mind, gathering of useful experiences, skills and knowledge.

Every other thing you need is the responsibility of your parents or guardian. In the situation where you have no parent or guardian, you are left with no option but to take up the challenge. With enough determination, you will be able to take care of yourself and also work on your mind as well.

What is common and can be done by anyone else does not deserve your time. Leave them for those who have more time to spare. The reason you have an uncommon brain is to enable you pursue the uncommon. For example, it is the thinking of any Israeli child to grow to do what no one has done before. And you must have similar mentality. Instead of being amazed by something, be fascinated. A determined mind that does not normally take a 'no' for an answer is crucial. It does not stop at anything until what is wanted is achieved. This is expected to be a part of the Ghanaian identity we want to create.

The way William Lee invented his hand knitting machine in the 15th century is a perfect example. Before then, knitting was done by hand. He imagined or saw a machine in his mind that could do the knitting better and faster than human hands. He said, '…The idea of my machine and creating it ate into my brain.' Everything he thought and dreamt about was the machine, and how to make it. He focused on it, worked at it, and eventually made it.

The desire to get something done, the desire to be who you really want to be, like William Lee, must 'eat' into your brain. Take a look around you. Look at the cars, phones, machines and anything artificial that you see. They all existed in the minds of people. People imagined them, thought about them, worked at them and finally created, and brought them into our physical world.

There are so many things in the world of your mind. Prepare yourself to search for them and bring them into the world to come and solve some of the problems in our dear country and world. It is normal to, for the first time, be scared by a lofty idea. But do not abandon it; write it down and keep pondering over it. You will eventually be able to work it out if you do not discard it.

There are so many astonishing feats the brain can accomplish. Follow the right path. Read books that will broaden your scope of imagination, observe your environment and learn from them. Take keen interest in learning from the animals and insects around you – study them because many of the lessons that have improved our world came from the plant and animal world. Hiking, camping, travelling and touring are very good for the brain as they provide rich experiences.

PART III

THE REQUIREMENTS FOR ACADEMIC EXCELLENCE

When students are equipped with the basic tools of language and mathematics, they are given an entrance into the world of learning. It becomes necessary to cultivate certain qualities in addition to the fundamentals of language and mathematics that will facilitate or serve as catalysts to the learning process. They are things without which the learning process becomes severely impaired or weak.

A READING CULTURE

Show me a family of readers, and I will show you the people who move the world.

Napoleon Bonaparte

'You got to read, baby, read. The more you read, the more you know. Knowledge is power and power is freedom and I want it,' said Harriet Ball, an American educator. There are two main ways to receive information: to listen, and to read. Since life is ruled by information, two of the best skills you need to learn are listening and reading skills.

People who fall short in these two areas experience huge learning challenges.

Even though these two are needed for effective learning, reading has an edge. The tools for listening are quite expensive. Additionally, they are not as readily available as compared to reading materials. It is also not easy to have the opportunity to be with many of the great people of the world in person. But books provide a better alternative. Therefore, it is a great privilege to have the ability to read.

When you see any student who loves reading, you have seen someone who is on the path of success. When reading becomes labour to people, they are bound to exit this world with many of the potentials in them untapped. The fuel of life is knowledge. And nothing makes knowledge readily accessible as reading does. It is what makes the scholar, a scholar. As a result, it is not something that the scholar or student can choose whether or not to do—it is a necessity.

To stop reading, as a student, is to stop learning. To be lazy in reading is to be a lazy student. And to be a poor reader is to be a poor student. It is reading that greases the wheel of knowledge. As a result, when reading stops, rust sets in. And if it continues, the wheel eventually grinds to a halt. When this happens, we get to where we have what some call 'educated illiterates'. Such people become a problem to society instead of being problem solvers. In business language, they become liabilities instead of being assets.

For a long time, the thinking of many students has been that reading is for General Art students. And this has caused a lot of problems as many such students did not see the need to read. Reading is for any student who desires quality education. Since knowledge enhances life, the best way to live well is to read well.

The ability to read and understand is a treasure for any student, and this must not go waste. The widespread attitude of dislike for reading among many people can be blamed on the lack of knowledge of what reading does to the life of a reader. A lot of students, who do not read, always give excuses for not doing so. And truly, there are other factors that account for that. But first of all, the desire and determination to read must be there. The saying goes that 'where there is a will, there is away.'

You are not only encouraged to love reading; you must influence your friends who do not like reading to also develop love for it. They are going to partner you in building a better country for us. If they do not read, they will create a lot of problems for you. Your work will be easier if you are surrounded by people who read a lot.

Any time you set your eyes on a book, there is a friendly voice behind it: 'come, let me tell you a secret.' There is this voice behind every book you see. Unfortunately, only few people hear this inviting and heart-warming voice. You surely have no idea what you miss if you go a whole day without reading anything.

No one understood this more than Pliny, the Elder. He read voraciously. It is said that in order to avoid any break in his reading, he had to listen to someone read for him even as he took his meal. That was quite extreme, but it shows what reading was to that man.

Mrs Auld, the wife of one of Frederick Douglass' slave masters, decided to teach Frederick to read and this is what her angry husband said: 'Learning will spoil the best nigger in the world. Now if you teach the nigger how to read, there will be no keeping him. It would forever unfit him to be a slave. He would at once become unmanageable and of no value to his master.' According to him, this man and his wife always monitored him to ensure that he never read. And he was always punished anytime he was caught reading.

Frederick Douglas did not have any formal training or education. But with assistance from his friends who were in school and his own effort, he taught himself to read. Without question, it was his ability to read that helped change his life. He paid himself out of slavery and with the knowledge he acquired, he became instrumental in the fight against slavery. He remarked, 'Once you learn to read, you will be free forever.'

Due to ignorance, even if students are paid to read, some will find a way to get the money without reading. It is said that Abraham Lincoln travelled several distances to go and borrow books to read. Howard Berg, the world's fastest reader, in his attempts to escape the attacks of robbers in his neighbourhood, resorted to safety at the library. There, he started to read. And when he fell in love with reading, he never stopped.

There are books available at various school libraries that must be made use of. But there have been instances where some students completed their senior high school studies without ever visiting their school libraries. As for you, you need it very well. Not only do you need your school's library, you need the community library as well.

Reading has no substitute in your academic and future work life. You must know that at any point in time, the one who reads more than you do, knows more than you know and therefore, is ahead of you. To be able to reach similar level of enlightenment with someone, you need to read as much as that person reads. And you must read more than someone reads to be above them. Take note that you can always be held a slave by anyone who is superior to you in knowledge. To avoid this, read!

Olaudah Equiano, also known as Gustavus Vassa, while relating his experience in England at his slave master's end, showed how he always studied the culture of his master and his child. He wrote, 'I had often seen my master and Dick employed in reading.' Reading was their family culture or way of life, and that was strange to Equiano. In fact, if he had gone to other homes, he may have seen similar culture.

When asked how to get smarter, Warren Buffett pointed to a stack of books and said, '…read 500 pages like this every week.' The question is this man is not a teacher or lecturer; he is a businessman, and so what did he need that extensive reading for? 'This is how knowledge builds up, like compound interest,' was his conclusion. A friend of his, Charlie Munger also said, 'We read a lot. I don't know anyone who is wise who doesn't read a lot.'

Dr Ben Carson, in his book *Gifted Hands*, writes how his mother stopped him and his elder brother Curtis from watching television and forced them to read because she realized that was what her white master's children did in their home. Before that, what those boys did after school was play and watch television. For that reason, they were always among the worst performing students in their respective classes. But when they started reading, the tables turned in their favour.

You have got to develop love for reading because you need it so much. Just as blocking your windpipe starves you of oxygen, with the resultant effect of death or brain damage, the refusal to read starves you of knowledge, with the resultant effect of a weak mind and poor performance in several areas of life. Reading will expose you to a wide range of experiences and improve your personality. It sits you on a round table with higher brains.

Reading enables you to interact with great personalities that you have never met or may never meet personally. The love for reading will give you an edge above your equals. The average student will read only the prescribed textbooks, but the excellent student will need to read beyond them.

Make good use of the school, community or city libraries. Go from town to town, house to house, if possible, in search of books to read. Go to the book stores around, and get yourself more books to read. Make sure you read all the books in your parents' library. Read everything readable, provided they have no harmful contents. On this note, it is advisable to seek the consent of your parents before reading some kind of books as certain books may not be good for you.

Spend more time on quality and relevant books. Mark Twain said, 'The man who does not read good books is no better than the man who can't.' To read any book at all is to eat any food at all. And you know that is dangerous. Read different kinds of books. Science students must read a lot of science fiction books. Read biographical books of accomplished people, especially those in your field of interest or study. Convert your television and video game playing time to reading.

Frequent television viewing must be discouraged. You see, the TV is also called an idiot box. The root of that may be very interesting, but obviously there is no need to spend much time with an idiot. Unless you are watching something positive, do not waste time on the television. It is more expensive watching television than the money your parents spend buying one.

Read more novels and fictions, especially the general and visual art students. They will heighten your creativity and activate your imagination. The roles assigned to the various characters will teach you more about the human nature and life in general. Non-fiction works will furnish you with specific information to address specific needs. Read more African stories to have a better picture of Africa, so that you can appreciate African challenges and dream of ways to help solve them.

It was said that 'if you want to hide something from the black man, put it in a book.' Now, there must be no place for them to hide anything. If you have siblings and friends who do not like reading, it must bother you. Explain to them and encourage them to read. It takes quality education to develop a country, but without a reading culture, the chances of quality education are very slim.

BELIEF IN SELF

What matters is not the idea a man holds but the depth at which he holds it.

Ezra Pound

One of our greatest endowments as human beings is the capacity to believe. Whatever people do or become in life is measurable to what they believe and the depth of their belief. The word *believe* is an amazing word. Anything that ever got done did so as a result of this special word. That which never got done was because that word was absent. It changes almost everything.

One of the major challenges we face in our schools is that many of our students lack self-confidence; especially, those who cannot express themselves well in English. It is true that friends may be laughing at you when you make grammatical slips. But the best thing to do is to boldly continue to express yourself and speak; despite the mistakes. Keep talking and let them keep laughing. You do not lose anything when you are laughed at. But you lose self-confidence when you stop expressing yourself because of that.

Fortunately, for those who lack self-confidence, there are some things that can be of help. The first thing is to have a positive mind-set. There is the need to reject all negative comments and speak positively to yourself. Look through a mirror and say nice things to yourself. You do not just need to say them, but believe in what you say to yourself. Also, making new friends can help. New friends may give you different challenges, especially the extroverts. Give yourself new challenges that will require more effort from you. Finally, dressing well and appearing presentable also boosts confidence.

You have no reason not to believe in yourself because you are equally gifted as anyone else. Somebody is a science wizard, another person is a business wizard, the other person is a visual art wizard and you are a football wizard. Who is inferior here? Everybody has their strength and weakness so why should your weakness make you lose your self-confidence? It is dangerous to lose self-confidence because that will make you sink in life. To keep floating, you must believe in yourself.

Glenn Cunningham, an American athlete, suffered a very fatal accident at the age of eight. That same incident left his younger brother dead. The doctors recommended amputating his legs since they were severely damaged. In fact, the transverse arch of the legs that supports the weight of the body was destroyed so the doctors predicted he was not going to be able to walk normally again even if he survived. Glenn refused to have his legs amputated. He told his mum that he was not only going to walk, he would run!

But Glenn knew what he wanted. After about two years, he made his first attempt to walk. He struggled, but kept believing. His walking improved and he attempted running. He kept going and started competing in races. In 1936, he set a world record winning the 800 meters race. The question is how was that possible? He believed it was possible, and it became so. When someone believes in something strongly enough, getting it done is certain.

Belief in self is not pride. It is not projecting self above others, or seeing one's self to be the only one person without whom nothing will work well. It is the absolute confidence that you are capable of achieving whatever you want. Believing in self is a basic requirement for personal development. If you do not believe in yourself, you end up making unnecessary mistakes, and pave the way for others to take advantage of you.

To succeed in life, there are so many initiatives you have to take, but if you do not have confidence in yourself, you will not take them. You end up always waiting for people to take the lead before you follow. If you do not believe in yourself, you cannot expect others to believe in you.

You do not have to be timid and feel inferior even if you have a profound weakness, because everyone has their own weaknesses. Believe and appreciate your uniqueness. Always remember that there is something in you that is made for greatness. Belief in self must not lead to pride. It is not only an act of pride to think that you are greater than someone else; it is also a sign of ignorance.

Know that you are not greater than anyone, and that no one is greater than you are as well. You are greater than only one thing: your former self. Therefore, compete against no one except your former self. At any point in time, you must ensure that you are better than who you used to be. And never see yourself as inferior in the midst of any group of people, irrespective of who they are and where they come from. They are who they are, and you are who you are!

It is not healthy at all to compare one's self to others. When such comparison is done, one of three things will be seen. One, you may see them doing better than you are. Two, you may see yourself doing better than they. And three, you may see yourself on the same plane with them. Now these are the effects:

When you see them doing better than you, chances are you will envy them. You will also lose self-confidence when you are in their company. When you see yourself doing better than they, chances are you will be arrogant and not give them the respect due them. This will make you obnoxious. The end is that they will hate you. And when you see yourself doing well as they are doing, you may think you have arrived. You may think that is the maximum you can go.

So the picture is very clear. It is not advisable to do that at all. The last thing you should do is to compare yourself to others. Concentrate on yourself and be the best you can be. There is no way you can be at your best self if you compare yourself to others. When others become the best they can be and you become the best you can be, then together you can make society and the country the best they can be.

THE QUALITY OF BEING OBSERVANT

Accuracy of observation is the equivalent of accuracy of thinking.

Wallace Stevens

Observation can be defined as the active acquisition of information using the senses. It is interesting to note that there is science behind all forms of knowledge derived from formal learning. This makes the skill of observation central. It is a skill without which the whole learning process is weakened or hampered.

One of the key benefits of observation is that it generates questions. And the more you ask questions, the more you learn. It also improves focus. Life is full of patterns and relationships. Focus is needed to be able to see these patterns and relationships. With these patterns and relationships, new ideas can be generated to solve problems. This skill, if built and developed, will help greatly even in your future career. It will also help improve your social life.

There are several ways to improve your observation skills. Normally, every big thing starts small. It is therefore difficult to try to understand it looking at the whole or big picture. Therefore, the best way to focus is to pay attention to the little things that make it up. This means in learning to observe, attention is paid to little things or details.

For a start in the observation process, a decision must always be made as to what should be your point of interest. This is because there are so many things that can catch your attention. Within a minute, the eyes and the other senses can recognize many things. You need to decide on one and ignore the rest. When you look at many things at once, it is almost impossible to properly observe any of them.

Focus on what is immediate or close to you. It is not the best to overlook or ignore what is close and then direct your attention to what is at a distance. The things that are nearest to you have the most immediate and greatest effect on you. Get a notepad or a diary, and regularly make entries of what you observe. Use words that give accurate description of the observation you make. This will help you identify even slight or minute changes in whatever you are monitoring.

Through observation, a farmer drew Simcha Blass' attention to a big tree growing in his backyard. No other tree survived within that area apart from that tree. Simcha became curious. He dug around the tree and discovered that close to the tree was a leaking pipe which supplied it with water. And through this discovery, Simcha and his son invented what is called the drip irrigation system.

Anyone who took things for granted could not have done that. Since nothing happens without a cause, anyone equipped with the skill of observation stands the chance of a good understanding of the happenings around them. And with this, they normally always know what to do. And more importantly, a lot of things do not take them by surprise.

It is very dangerous to take what happens around you for granted as it cannot be predicted what they may develop into. Even when you knock your feet against an object, take a few moments to ask questions. This may sound stupid, but it is a good practice. Make sure you are always aware of who is close to you, and what is around you wherever you find yourself. When you see somebody or a stranger in your vicinity repeatedly, you must be curious. Wherever you find yourself, take a few seconds or minutes to scan and assess the environment before you settle. This is not to make you suspicious, but smart and not indifferent.

'Enjoy every step you take. If you're curious, there is always something new to be discovered in the backdrop of your daily life.' said Roy T. Bennett. The skill of being observant works hand in hand with curiosity. Attempts can only be made to change something if enough is known about it. Therefore, you can only change and improve your environment if you know more about it and understand how it works.

Observation sets the tone for curiosity, which is an essential posture for knowledge acquisition. You can learn something new every day if you are curious enough. Ask questions about whatever you do not understand; keep asking and searching until you have a satisfying answer. More importantly, learn to ask *why*?

If something is done, there must be a reason. And there is a reason if it is not done. It is not enough to remember that something is not done. It is better to know and remember *why* it is not done. Take keen interest in whatever happens around you and eschew indifference.

Questions are like guides, so learn to ask questions. It takes someone who shows concern to ask questions about something or a situation. Ask and keep asking; ask teachers, even foreigners, visit libraries and search the internet for answers. It is said that it was the incident of an apple falling from a tree that made Sir Isaac Newton discover the law of gravity.

But the falling of apples and other objects are common. Seeing objects fall from various heights has never been anything strange. So what made Sir Newton behave that way? Obviously, he was a life-long learner and someone on a mission. To such people, nothing is ignored and everything is of interest. In fact, if Newton had considered it normal and not asked questions, he would not have made that discovery.

If things are normal, there must be reasons they are so. Can something that is not normal later be normal? Why can it not be normal? It is not good to be quick to accept or refuse what people say, so ask questions about whatever you see in your community and the country as a whole, and you will make startling discoveries.

There are so many things we think are right that may actually be wrong. And there are also many things we think are wrong that may actually be right. The question is how do we know? By asking quality questions, of course!

INDEPENDENT THINKING SKILLS

Where all think alike, no one thinks very much.

Walter Lippman

The skill of independent thinking is also one of the several foundational skills needed to receive quality education. It is a skill set needed to convince or be persuaded in your own mind that something is good or bad, to convince yourself that the information you receive or are receiving is true, reasonable or false. What this means is that you do not accept something to be true because your friend or peer says it is, but because you are convinced it is true based on your own judgment.

There are reasons this skill set is very important. It nurses the trait of thinking outside the box—something that unlocks creativity. It also builds a sense of responsibility. In other words, it makes people take responsibility for what they do and not blame them on others. Similarly, it builds self-confidence.

There are a few things that can help build this skill. You need to do independent work and not copy the work of friends. The exercises of other students reflect their thinking and the way they understand things. One of the reasons exercises or assignments are given is to assess the thinking of individual students and not the thinking of the whole class. And this is why copying the work of friends is a terrible thing to do in class. It is important to show your own thinking and how you understand things to your teacher, not to present that of others as yours. When you are given exercises or assignments, your answer may not be accepted by some teachers, but try to answer them your own way rather than just getting some books or sources to copy the answers.

Do not depend heavily on the information you get anywhere else. Scrutinize them and make your own decision on them. If possible, modify them to suit your desired outcome. Try new experiences. Read about people of different cultures and backgrounds. Tolerate divergent views. And learn to do things on your own without being instructed or supervised.

Independent thinking is so important that the absence of it or any significant weakness with it will turn the mission of education upside down. Though the traditional way of thinking normally defines a group of people, it is important for individuals to think differently as and when the situation demands.

All the things that have improved our world were made when people thought outside the box or independently. They were made by people who looked at things from different perspectives. Doing things the same way and expecting different results is a problem. Quality learning is born out of series of discoveries. But these are not possible when people are caged in prescribed thinking patterns. It is educationally suicidal when people are confined to the thinking pattern into which they were born.

Michael Morrish visited Ghana and in his book *Development in The Third World* he commented on the traditional buildings or houses he saw in a part of Ghana. This is what he said: '…in building their houses, they use methods that have been handed down from one generation to the next.' This means as far as buildings are concerned, those people never think outside the box. The result of this is that until they decide to entertain individual thinking regarding building, their buildings will continue to remain the same until the world is no more.

Our societies normally do things as were handed down to us. And this is not necessarily bad in itself. But it must be admitted that it is not the best way to go. This kind of lifestyle deprives society of innovation. The very things there are in society are what were discovered from the thinking and experiences of those who came earlier. They are not the only things that can ever be. They are only foundational. They are to be depended upon for further discoveries.

It is essential for people to remember their roots, but they are not to remain their roots; they are to go beyond their roots to uncharted territories. Our forebears had reasons for doing whatever they did and in the way they did them. Their reasons must serve only as a guide. People who have different aspirations do not do things the same way. Since there are challenges these days that never existed in the past, dwelling on the past way of thinking will make current challenges overwhelming.

Equip yourself with what will enable you address challenges in ways different from how everybody does them. It must be remembered that that single way everybody does something is not the only way it can be done. There is almost always a different way to solve any human problem. It is wrong to think that because something has not been attempted, it is impossible. Think outside the box.

Thomas Edison read a lot of Sir Isaac Newton's science books and found Newton's work very complex. It was so hard for him that he could not relate to what Newton was trying to say—he could not derive any meaning out of them. He decided to ignore Newton's approach and study them his own way. And after persistent attempts, he succeeded with his own theories and came up with all those wonderful inventions that are still operational in the world today.

In fact, if he had depended on Newton's approach, he may not have been able to do all that he did. The reality is that he thought differently from what Newton thought. They both worked around the same concept, but adopted different approaches. To know what Newton knew, you have to think what Newton thought. But to do what Newton did not do, you must think what Newton did not think.

It must be noted that everything contained in the books in the world is not all there is to be known. Like a guide in a lost forest, they only lead you to the right path and leave you there to continue on your own. The books and textbooks being studied are only what people have learnt. The authors only attempt to provide an exposition on what they know so that others could benefit from them and also continue from there.

It is a serious problem if a student does not know anything else apart from what is learnt from teachers and books. Until one's knowledge goes beyond book knowledge, they are not properly educated. If you are not able to create your own version of what you have received from books and from teachers, you have not studied yet. The best way to test if you really understand what a teacher has taught you is to put that down in your own words, or come up with examples of your own as said earlier. But this can only be arrived at if you think independently.

TEAM SPIRIT

Great discoveries and improvements invariably involve the cooperation of many minds.

Alexander Graham Bell

Have you ever wondered why cargo trucks and other trucks that carry extremely heavy loads have many wheels or tires? The weights of the heavy loads they cart are distributed among the number of wheels. This does not only make it possible for the truck to carry the load, it preserves the roads as well. Great things are done when many things work together as a unit.

The principle of cooperation does not only apply to machines, it does apply much more to humans. It is a prerequisite for both individual and national development. Many things go wrong for individuals and society when team spirit or cooperation is absent among people. In fact, so many things will never be possible without it.

This shows that the skill of teamwork is needed if you should be a well-rounded student or intellectual. In any field of learning, teamwork is needed for optimal learning. As you climb the academic ladder, you will need to work with other scholars to handle certain projects. There are many concepts or things that you will understand better if you work together with your friends.

You were not made to live or walk alone. It is almost impossible to find anything in the universe working in isolation. In basic science, we are taught what is called symbiosis. This is organisms working together for mutual benefits. And it is virtually what teamwork is all about. Every single human being you meet has something that you do not have and knows something that you do not know, no matter how little. If you doubt, check their thumbprints.

The lack of knowledge of the need for teamwork makes people commit a lot of mistakes in society. It is a mistake to underrate or despise someone. This mistake deteriorates to the level where people begin to envy others and even attempt to destroy them. Do you know that anytime someone dies, a vacancy is created? Yes, society is robbed of their unique potentials.

The greatest resource to any country is its people, not the natural resources. Countries can develop without these natural resources, but they cannot develop without their people. Through teamwork, the human resource of society is harvested for development. Selfishness and the urge to work in isolation do a lot of harm to individuals and society.

For illustration, try this exercise: Try and ignore the rest of your fingers. And attempt eating with only one finger. How does it look like; is it easy? This is what happens when because of envy and greed or lack of knowledge, people refuse to work as a team and destroy their colleague(s).

As termites work together to build their mounds, and bees their hives; human beings work together to create societies or civilizations, and to improve life. Nature teaches the need for teamwork and gives remarkable examples to drive this point home.

Take, for instance, a colony of black ants. When one identifies a source of food, the others will be signalled. The colony will come and fetch the food. In the open space, they are threatened by any fluid. When it rains and there is a mad rush of water or flood, they all quickly form a mesh and float as a mass. So instead of them being dispersed into individuals and get destroyed, the flood carries them away as a mass to a different location and there, they start life again. None of them is destroyed, and the whole colony gets saved. Is it not beautiful? This is the power of teamwork.

To help build your team-working spirit, take advantage of any team-working environment. Some of these environments are the various sports teams, music and drama groups, the clubs and cadet group, the class groups for various projects and assignments. These groups open up great opportunities to develop team-working skills.

Ensure you always attend group meetings. At any such meeting, discharge the duty the group assigns you fully. Learn to listen attentively to any team member who may have the floor to make any submission. When any weakness is identified on the part of any team member, effort must be made to help overcome it. The reason is that the weakness of a team member is the team's weakness.

When your team engages in any discussion, do not be there only to write and listen to those who will talk. Always contribute to the discussion. Never be afraid to speak, thinking that you may be wrong or make grammatical errors. Make your point anyway, and say whatever you have to say. Also, do not disregard any question or statement a team member makes—there may be some substance in what they may say.

Again, one of the principal things to help your team-working skill is to remember that any Ghanaian student you see is your team member, whether they are from your school or a different school. Any boy or girl you see, whether you know them or not, is your colleague in nation building. They are going to partner with you to make the country and world better.

Therefore, any Ghanaian you meet is important to you and the country as a whole. You need them just as they need you. There is no end to what can be achieved if you learn team-working. When different individuals bring what they all can do best together, they make a wonderful society.

This is what Warren Buffett said of his business partner: 'I can see; he can hear. We make a great combination.' You can do one thing and your friend can do something else; work as a team and reach greater heights. You should be able to work to a point and be ready to allow someone else to come and complete it. Doing this should not be a problem at all.

Some of the benefits of teamwork are that it brings out the best in individuals. It reduces selfishness and unhealthy individual competitions. It creates satisfaction in accomplishments rather than in rewards. And this trait is crucial to nation building. The service rendered to society must be more valuable than the reward or praise that come with them.

After World War II, Harry Truman's secretary of state, George Marshall, presented a seventeen billion dollar European Recovery Program, which was designed to reconstruct Europe after that huge destruction. Considering the international reputation America would receive as a result of such a plan, Harry Truman's advisors encouraged him to call this exercise the 'Truman Plan'; thus, naming it after himself because he was the President.

But he declined and asked that it be named the 'Marshall Plan' after the one who created it. And this is what Harry Truman often said, 'It is remarkable how much could be accomplished when you don't mind who receives the credit.' This is a sign of someone who understood teamwork. There has always been a team behind any significant achievement in the world and there will always be.

PROPER UNDERSTANDING OF TIME

Waste your money and you're out of money, but waste your time and you have lost a part your life.

Michael Leboeuf

This is one area a lot of people are very poor at. And it is quite astonishing looking at the effect of the misuse of time on lives. The damages caused by the misuse of time are almost irreparable. As a result, one of the best assets people can get for themselves is a proper training towards the use of time. For you, as a student, it is priceless.

What is time like? It is scientifically defined as what a clock or a watch measures, but there is more to it. Everybody is aware of it yet, it is difficult to understand it in its entirety. When time is taken out, there will be nothing on earth. In fact, there will not even be any earth in the first place. Whatever is seen with the naked eyes begins and ends with time. Everything done on earth is marked by time.

The effect of time cuts across every facet of life; making it one of the most complicated things humans have to deal with. As a result, to reach a good level of understanding of time is to reach a greater level of understanding of life. So a foundation for proper attitude to the use of time is a must. Considering the place of time in life, the most significant change in a person's life is their change of attitude towards time. Even the slightest positive change will yield a significant result.

Two things lead to the misuse of time: indiscipline and poor education. Normally, people's approach to time is their approach to life. It is unthinkable to imagine or see time going waste. To plan the use of your time is to plan your life. And no one is in control of their lives if they cannot control the use of their time.

The changes things undergo are so minute that it is very hard and almost impossible to see them happening in the process. They are only seen or noticed when they are significant enough. And even with that, they are seen after they have already taken place. Time offers the best tool to monitor the change process.

What is worth taking note of is that any microsecond gone is an index of a change within you and around you. In this regard, it appears that the analogue watches serve better than the digital ones; as by their ticking sounds, they draw attention to the change that we would otherwise not be aware of.

If you lose the money your parents give you for school, never worry much. But if you do lose or waste your time, you must miss a pulse; it should be a matter of concern to you. The reason is that there is no such thing as extra time in real life. Once it is past, it remains so. You cannot afford to waste this precious commodity. It must be properly managed.

The saying goes, 'time is money'. Do you have any idea why it is said so? This statement is made in terms of the concept of currency. Currency is a medium of exchange. Like money, time is also a medium of exchange. What people become or get in life is what they exchange their time for. It is mistakenly thought that the barter system of trade is over. But this is false! You are always engaging in barter trade with your time.

People engage in barter trade every single day. And the practice shall continue until the world is no more. Whenever you see people, whether young or old, idling and chatting, they are doing a barter trade! For instance, if they do that for about two hours, they have only exchanged two hours of the time, which is their life, for some gratification that comes out of idling and chatting. When someone spends half a day on the phone or in front of the television, they have engaged in a barter trade.

Having had a better picture of what time is, it is important to be abreast of the ways of managing it for maximum output. First of all, take a little time to consider what you spent your time on in the last three or four days. What did you do in the mornings, afternoons, evenings, nights and dawns? This should give you a good picture of how you have been using your time. If it is good exchanging your time for those things, improve upon it; if not, change is the way to go.

One of the first things to do in helping manage time is to plan. This plan should start with an overall dream. By this dream, reference is made to what you want your life to be. Then you narrow it down to the little things or specifics that will take you to the dream land. This will give you yearly, monthly, weekly, and daily plans. This means what you do daily will give you your weekly outcome, what you do weekly will give your monthly outcome and so on.

Though all these plans are necessary, the most important of them all are your daily plans. The success of people's plans has always depended heavily of the success of their daily plans. This emphasizes how little things matter. Specific times should be set for daily activities. For example, my mathematics assignment will be done from 5pm-6.25pm on Wednesday.

It is waste of time to keep sitting down to learn when you are tired. What to do is to have some regular breaks. For example, you can take a break every 40 or 45 minutes. This will reenergize you and help your concentration. It is better to spend five or ten minutes to refuel than to sit for hours without fuel in your tank. Also, do not allow your friends to disrupt your plans. Entertain and hang around with friends when your time for that is up. If you can spare someone a minute or two of your time to do them good do not hesitate, but make sure you cover up after that.

Reduce or stay away from distractions. Do you realize that anything that attracts your attention takes your time? Yes, it does. Such things do not only take your time, they deplete the energy of your brain as well. One of the ways of conserving electricity in the house is to switch off lights and other electrical gadgets when they are not really needed. The same works for the brain. To concentrate the energy of the brain, limit the things recognized by the senses. This means the learning environment must be simple.

In carrying out any activity on your daily plan, certain things may distract you. In the house, for instance, your phone must be switched off if it has nothing to do with what you are studying, or you may put it away from you.

Those who have study rooms at home must make good use of them. If there is no study room at home and the condition in the house is not conducive, the public library will be of help. In school if the classroom is noisy, go to the library or any quiet place. And learn to politely say no to anything that interrupts your schedule.

There are times in the day that you may not be able to use a particular chunk of time the way you have planned it. For example, you may be on a long journey, you may be trapped in a terrible traffic situation on your way somewhere, or you may be compelled to wait for someone at a place for hours, etc. In order not to waste such moments, you can use a period like that to read a book, ponder over a topic in class that did not go well with you, or explore any new challenge or idea that that situation may provoke. Under 'normal' circumstances, we get sad, angry, murmur and complain when things like that happen. But these do not help the situation in any way.

Make room for the unexpected too. Time management cannot be fully discussed without considering good health. As important as time is, without good health, time is either useless or a torment. Good health is needed to make investments in time. Therefore, you do not have to gamble with your health. People tend to ignore the value of good health until they are seriously sick. You must make conscious effort to take good care of your health, and abstain or desist from anything that poses a threat to it.

The things that make for good health must be taken note of and implemented religiously. Paramount among these is a healthy diet. It is true that hunger is not a good thing, and it is not a joke to be seriously hungry. But it is dangerous to be in a hurry to eat since that may not give you time to observe the protocols of hygiene. Eating or dinning is a serious business—therein lies health and sickness, healthy brain and weak brain.

How food is eaten is as important as what is eaten. It is possible to poorly eat a good meal. For example, if the hands, after exposure to many things, are not properly washed with soap and water before eating, the good meal could be contaminated. The common practice has been that people wash their hands with water alone before eating. But after eating, they wash hands with soap. But the hands must be washed properly with soap and water before eating.

On the issue of good meals, it is normally thought that a good meal is that which tastes good. Frankly, meals that do not taste good are very difficult to eat. But when attention is paid to taste, only the tongue is satisfied while the rest of the body stay largely neglected. So meals must be taken on account of what they give the body and not necessarily how 'tasty' they may be.

For example, among students, salmon should be preferred to chicken since it contains a good amount of omega 3, which is very good for the brain. But in the situation where the quest to satisfy the tongue is paramount, students are more likely to prefer chicken to salmon. Therefore, there is the need to eat well, observe personal hygiene and exercise regularly to stay healthy. Though it is important to avoid wasting time, there must be some level of flexibility in your plans and actions, since rigidity will wear you down.

PART IV

PILLARS OF QUALITY LEARNING

As there are columns and pillars that carry the loads or weights of buildings, there are certain things that perform similar function in quality learning. It will be difficult to achieve certain learning outcomes without them. This chapter takes a look at some of them.

SELF-DISCOVERY

All my life I had been looking for something, and everywhere I turned someone tried to tell me what it was. I accepted their answers too, though they were often in contradiction and even self-contradictory. I was naïve. I was looking for myself and asking everyone except myself questions which I, and only I, could answer. It took me a long time and much painful boomeranging of my expectations to achieve a realization everyone else appears to have been born with: That I am nobody but myself.

Ralph Ellison

The Merriam-Webster dictionary of English defines self-discovery as the act or process of achieving self-knowledge. This clearly sets self-discovery as a fundamental element of learning. And it is true in the sense that all manner of learning begin with the known to the unknown. In other words, we depend on the immediate to reach the distant. But what can be more immediate to any individual than the self?

One of the primary things children learn is to know their own names. For example, you mistakenly call a three-year old child by a wrong name and the immediate response is, 'no, my name is...' They learn to distinguish self from others or other things. At primary school, you wrote about yourself. You did not do that exercise for the sake of doing it. It formed part of the beginning of your learning process. It showed how much information you had about yourself. Since you are now older than you were four or five years ago, you should know more about yourself now than you knew then. On a piece of paper, can you write two or three things you now know about yourself that you did not know some time ago? Before you go further, stop and ask yourself this question: who am I? The answers to this question will show you to what extent you know yourself. You may write your answer and share them with your parents.

Self-discovery has a lot of importance. It builds the sense of inquiry. For example, you want to do and have certain things in life. But why do you like item B and not A? Why am I always quite or noisy, why should I know why I am always quite or noisy? With self-discovery, you frequently want to know and understand yourself. This sense of inquiry is vital because the same is needed in your academic work.

Life is simply interaction between self and the environment. Since the end of all learning is to make life better, a good knowledge of self and the environment is all that academic learning is about. Because of this, any level of ignorance of self is a hindrance to education.

Normally, the way individuals respond to the matters regarding themselves, influences how they respond to things around them. And people who always try to know and understand themselves will equally do the same to their environment or things around them as such things influence them in many ways. For example, some knowledge of self is needed to interpret information or data received from the environment. And in the same way, some knowledge of the environment is needed to interpret information received from self. They are interrelated.

One of the first lessons to draw from self-discovery is to realize your uniqueness. It is necessary to know that you are unique. The world's human population runs to billions, but no two people are ever the same, not even identical twins. You are one and only; you do not have a duplicate. The proof of this is your fingerprint—your fingerprint differs from that of any individual on earth.

And as said earlier, since no individual is superior to anyone, it will be a mistake to be dissatisfied with yourself and seek to be like someone else. The way you see yourself is shaped by the information you have of your own self and what you receive from the environment. You need to make sure you do not misinform yourself. Do not accept the negative and wrong words that are frequently used in your environment. For example, the word *ordinary* as normally used to describe some people is very destructive—do not accept it for yourself and never use it for anyone.

We may have an ordinary house, car or lifestyle, but we cannot have an ordinary human being. No human being is ordinary even if they are invalid. You cannot be ordinary because you are a human being. You may not be among those considered the best students in your class, but you are not ordinary, and you can never be. Yes, they may be the 'best', but the best in what? That is where the fact lies. They are the best in a certain area, and you are in another area.

It is difficult for a human being to be ordinary. The only way for an individual to be ordinary is for them to think so (that they are ordinary). The ancient philosopher, Parmenides, said, 'whatever is, is.' This also means that what is not is not. Therefore, what is ordinary is ordinary, and what is not ordinary, is not ordinary—as simple as that.

There is no way someone who does not know how something is can better define it. And this applies to you. You know and should know yourself more than anyone else does of you. It is a great mistake to be worried because of somebody's opinion of you. Therefore, don't let the untrue comments made by those who don't know you bother you at all. People's opinions must belong to them, and you must be yourself.

You may not look attractive as some people may expect, but that does not make you less human. The reason you do not look attractive to them is that you do not need to look attractive to them. You only need to look attractive to yourself and to those who love you. And fortunately, for you and those who love you, you are very beautiful; to such people, you are always special. And that is what matters. No one can be ugly to those who really love them.

Furthermore, you are not somebody's photocopy; not even the photocopies of your parents. One of the challenges against self-discovery is the misunderstanding about role models. Role models are very essential, but the quest is not to be the second version of your role model. Your role models are their unique selves, and you are your unique self. You only learn lessons from them to build yourself. Normally, society makes people who excel in their fields of endeavour the standard for the up and coming ones. For example, in football, any good player is Messi or Ronaldo.

In academia, any good science student is Einstein or Newton.

Miserably, we tend to feel pampered and great when compared to successful people. In fact, it is good to feel great, but there is nothing to feel great about in such unhealthy comparison. Frankly, Albert Einstein would never like to be compared to any great scientist who came before him. Ronaldo or Messi would not want to be called by the name of any great player who played before them, so why should you or anyone else?

People may call you so many names and that is their opinion. Never allow their words to influence your opinion of yourself. All human beings are unique in their own ways, and no single individual is a standard for another. The academic skill that Albert Einstein displayed is not the height of academic excellence; you can even do better than Einstein if only you so desire.

Another advantage of self-discovery is that it prevents the mistake of living a false life. It makes you live your own life and not the life of someone else. You do not have to look down on your individuality no matter how odd you think something about you is; just polish and shape it up for your good and that of the country. This is better put in the words of Mandy Hale: 'So you're a little weird? Work it! A little different? OWN it! Better to be a nerd than one of the herd!' You may come from a poor home, but that does not define you. Your real self, your individuality, is hidden inside your outer body.

ROLE MODELS

A role model is defined as a person looked up to as an example. And an example is a parallel or that which makes for clarity and proper understanding of something. There is almost nothing new in the world. Whatever anyone may want to do, someone has already done or is doing the same or similar. Almost any path one wants to tread has been trodden by someone else in one way or the other. What this means is that there are people who have done or are doing what you would love to do.

Many such people have done and are doing them successfully. They are the people considered as role models or good examples. Role models play a very important part in developing and shaping individual personalities. Your role model would help you to believe in yourself. From your role models, it is easy to believe that once they have done it, you can also do it.

A life without a role model is like travelling without any specific destination in mind. In the same way, learning without a role model will make the search for quality education almost impossible. It is hard to find an excellent student who does not have a role model. One of the ways to do well in class, if you are not, is to get a good role model.

Getting a good role model would lead you into asking questions that would compel a change in your life. For example, after settling on someone as your role model, you may ask questions such as: *How did they grow up into who they are now? What did they do, and how did they do them? How did they behave when they were young? Do they have secrets? Are there any lessons I must learn from them?*

And because your desire is to succeed as they have succeeded, these questions are very important. The answers you get from these questions are enough to force a change of behaviour, draw your attention to some mistakes you may be making, or inspire you to work harder.

It is very important to get a quality role model at this early stage of your life in order to succeed as a student, and in your future life. You will draw a lot of inspiration from your role model that would help push yourself to your very best.

You can have several role models because there are several areas of your life that must be developed. For example, if your parents have not been successful with their education, they cannot be your role models in your schooling. But they may be very hard-working or morally upright. In such areas, they can be your role models.

You can have your role models from home, school, church or mosque, city or country. However, if those around you cannot meet your expectations, if they do not inspire you in any way, choose from outside. If those you choose are not close to you, you can listen to their audio tapes, watch their videos and read their books. And if they are alive, you may write to them as well.

To succeed as your role models have done, you must work as they have worked. You need quality role models in order to steer clear of poor peer influences. It would be very healthy to take many of your role models from advanced or developed countries so that you can help the country also attain their same level of development. Quality role models are essential to quality education. Take a little time to ponder on these questions: Who are your role models? Why are they your role models? How have they influenced your behaviour and attitude towards learning?

EMOTIONAL LITERACY

In knowing yourself very well, this area is of utmost importance. Actually, it is the bedrock of self-discovery. And this thing in question is what is called emotional literacy. It has to do with the emotional aspect of life. This is a very important area because how well people do in life and society depends, to a large extent, on how they handle their emotions. Being abreast of this area will not only help you discover yourself, but it will improve you as a person.

Emotional literacy is simply defined as the ability to recognize, understand and appropriately express one's emotions. In other words, emotional literacy is knowledge about the emotions. Sometimes, you feel happy. And at other times, you feel sad. What emotional literacy does is that it will help you to know, understand and express these feelings in ways that will be to your advantage and not to your disadvantage. Emotions are meant to work for us but not against us.

Now, what are emotions in the first place? The Oxford Dictionary of English defines emotion as a strong feeling deriving from one's circumstances, mood or relationships with others. Basically, they are feelings. And to borrow Mark Manson's words, they are the feelings that tell people to pay attention to something. What this means is that when you are angry, your attention is being drawn to something you do not like. Like a placard, anger holds that very ugly thing in front of you. Similarly, when you are happy, your attention is being drawn to something that needs to be cherished or celebrated.

Therefore, even though there are positive and negative feelings, they all serve useful purposes. What is important is how they are expressed. Emotions must be expressed and not suppressed. It is very dangerous to suppress emotions. So to avoid suppressing them, they must be expressed appropriately. In other words, they must be managed.

In managing emotions, language is very important. The right words are essential to managing emotions. First of all, in any emotional situation, you must identify the emotion by selecting the right word. Words send signals: the right word will send a correct signal, and the wrong word will send a wrong signal. Since signals must be interpreted, the wrong signal (word) will lead to a wrong interpretation.

The lesson here is that the way you interpret the signal received will determine the way you will act. Therefore, it is important to 'label your placard' correctly—choose the right word. For example, it is better for a girl to think of herself as *plump* than to think she is *fat*. Though the two words hold the same image, they trigger different interpretations. Therefore, the right language is paramount in dealing with your own or someone else' emotions.

The next important thing is the interpretation. Take for example, a friend of yours who has lied against you to some members of your class. Let us say because he or she is not a close friend, this deed makes you angry. Here, this anger only draws your attention to the lie this friend has told about you; this is what is on the placard. The next, is the interpretation. If you interpret this lie as something that will make your friends make fun of you, or see you as a bad person, you will only get mad at the person. But if you interpret it as a trap from that friend who wants to destabilize you emotionally and waste your precious time, you are likely to let go of it and remain focused.

There is another way of handling negative emotions like this. Though it is weird, it has been found to produce good results. Instead of doing all the thought processes in your mind, write them down. Writing about that emotion may help a lot. You will not use what you write for anything. But the clue is that it gives you some time, thus giving you some level of control over that emotion. And because writing requires thinking, or appeals to your thought process, you would become more rational and less emotional; hence, getting some command over the situation.

We have a great opportunity in handling our emotions. Luckily, in all emotional situations, nobody gives the interpretation; we give them ourselves. Therefore, we can always help ourselves by choosing what will favour us even if it does not make sense. If a senseless decision will keep you sane, it must be better than a sensible one that will make you lose your head.

On the other hand, there are some emotional situations that are very difficult to handle. In such cases, you need to talk to somebody for help. If you are not on vacation, you need to see the school's counsellor. But when you are at home, you must talk to your parents. Sadly, some young ones do not like talking to their parents about certain issues. Rather, they would talk to peers or friends. In fact, this is one of the characteristics of this stage of life. But it must not be encouraged; it is very bad. Whenever you get to the situation of not being comfortable to discuss any emotional issue with your parents, you are on a dangerous path. There should be nothing in your life that cannot be discussed with either your dad or mum. One of the best ways of managing your emotions is to talk about them with your parents.

Your parents must be your best friends. If your dad is too harsh, then mum must be your best friend; and if mum is not that type, then your dad must be. Discuss all your emotional issues with them. Discuss any struggles you are facing with them. If you have not done that before, give it a try and you will see that they are better friends than those you find among your peers. If your parents are not alive, any good family member or neighbour can serve you this purpose. With their support, you will excel in emotional literacy.

You can only know more about something by asking more questions about it. Ask questions about the emotion you are dealing with. For example, if something bad happens to you, you will have a negative emotion. All you need to do is to choose the right language to describe that emotion: are you *sad* or *disturbed*? Why should you be disturbed and not sad? Do you have any reason to be disturbed? Is there anything right that you can do in this mood? Is it possible to let go of this feeling? How can that be done? When should you do that?

You need to know why you do what you do, and why you do things the way you do them. Your parents can help with some good answers if you talk to them about your emotions. This is one of the ways emotional literacy works. It is emotional literacy that will make you ask questions like: why don't I like that bag? Is my reason for not liking that bag good enough? Why do I always go to town without exeat? What does this action speak of me? Will dad be happy to hear of this?

Emotional literacy will not only make you know yourself better, your behaviour will be improved since you always want to have sound reasons to do what you do. You will understand your friends and neighbours as well. It will help you to feel what they feel. And this will make you a more reasonable person.

Consider this scenario: Your parents buy for you the latest iPhone and because you are not allowed to take phones to school, you keep it at home when going to school. You open your bag on vacation and find out that it is not there. Your younger brother has spoilt it beyond repair. What would you do in such a situation?

There is a general way almost anyone will approach this situation. You will shout on top of your voice and call that miserable boy, wherever he may be, and beat the hell out of him. But you love your brother. And truly, you do not love the phone more than you love him, so why would you hurt the one that you love?

This is where emotional literacy will help. It will help you to approach the situation differently from the traditional way. Do not think emotional literacy will make you laugh over this situation, no. You will be angry, but not destructive. It will let you know that before they bought the phone for you, you were fine, so you can be fine if it is no more.

Emotional literacy will help you a lot. It will improve your academic performance, it will make you healthier and happier, it will improve your relationship with others, and it will keep you collected while others are losing their heads. True self-awareness cannot be possible without emotional literacy.

SOUND VALUES

The mystery of human existence lies not just in staying alive, but in finding something to live for.

Fyodor Dostoevsky

John Santrock defines values as beliefs and attitudes about how things should be. They are some of the building blocks that define the characters of people. The kinds of values people hold influence what they do and how they do them. Because of this, it is necessary to settle on the ones that would make you a better person, help you realize your dreams, and also help you contribute well to society.

This stage of life offers one of the best opportunities to build a sound personal value system. Whether you are going to do well or succeed in life depends largely on this. There must be certain things that define you. In other words, there should be things you stand for; they are your values. They serve as a sieve or filter for your behaviour so that if you do not have them, you easily end up doing anything you find convenient.

Normally, people pick up values from home. As a result, students who have very good parents stand the chance of getting sound values laid for them. It is a serious problem for students who have such opportunity to throw that opportunity away and rather resort to peers for their values.

This should be avoided. The values picked from the parents can be modified as one matures and learns to appreciate things for themselves.

Those who do not have such kind of parents are faced with great challenges as they are left with no option but to depend on their immediate environment for their values. And peers are the primary source they resort to in this situation. They normally end up with poor values since the environment almost always offers no hope for sound values.

It is a big challenge for those who do not have good parents or guardians to have strong values. Individuals form their values from the understanding of what life is and what they want to become in life. But at a very young age, it is not easy for people to understand what life is about, let alone knowing exactly what they want in life. This is the challenge of those who do not have parents or guardians; they have very limited experiences, and hardly know what exactly they want in life. This deprives them of what it takes to have sound values.

The following are sound values that you must have. They are needed to make you successful in school and will go a long way to take you to your dreams.

SELF-DISCIPLINE

I could only achieve success in my life through self-discipline, and I applied it until my wish and my will became one.

Nikola Tesla

Self-discipline is the trait of being well-behaved. It has to do with conducting yourself in ways that are consistent with best practices. Discipline ensures that you are at the right place at the right time, and also doing the right thing at the right place.

As humans, we cannot be at different places or carry out different activities at the same time. Because of this, at any point in time, we are either at the right place or the wrong place, either doing the wrong or the right thing. To help you, you need to take your time to ask these questions frequently anytime you become aware of what you may be doing: What am I doing? Is this in my plan for today?

The reason these questions are important is that we are prone to doing what is convenient. But what is convenient may not necessarily be what ought to be done. With such actions, their consequences are not normally taken into consideration. Therefore, the answers to questions like the above will either make us stop or continue with that.

Jim Rohn said that self-discipline is the bridge between goals and achievement. This means it is not enough to dream—certain things are needed to take you to your dreams. To allow for success in any endeavour, there must be a well-spelt out plan and a determination to follow through the plan. And self-discipline is what it takes to do things according to plan. A life without discipline is marked for failure no matter how promising it looks or begins. It is so crucial that it seems nothing really gets done without it.

Generally, human beings do not like any restrictions. We do not like anything that requires a little effort to do. And discipline is full of that. That is why a lot of people do not like it. It is almost a no-go area for adolescents. But it is one thing without which many of the things people have accomplished could not have been possible.

It must be admitted that the issues about discipline are easier said than done. It is possible to start being disciplined only to relapse in no time. The first step towards discipline is to understand your need to succeed. The next is to develop a deep hunger or desire to succeed in whatever you have set for yourself to achieve. It is this great hunger that will fuel and sustain your drive for discipline. And as much as possible, avoid the things that will make you undisciplined by forming better habits.

Those who succeed and make progress in what they do never have them on a silver platter. They battle with tough decisions and make a lot of sacrifices.

HARD WORK

Colin Powell said, 'There are no secrets to success. It is the result of preparation, hard work, and learning from failure.'

It is often said that hard work is the key to success. And there is a sense in that. Life is full of activities such that any slight moment of inactivity is almost equal to death.

Activities that are consciously carried out to achieve set targets or goals are termed work. But many targets would not yield so easily. Much effort and endurance are needed to push through in other to get them. And this is all hard work is about. It involves getting your sight set on your desired objective(s) and going through inconveniences to achieve them. It is the opposite of idleness or laziness.

Farmers take deliberate and painstaking effort to till the lands and tender their crops. So that the quantity and quality of their harvests depend on the amount of time spent and quality work done on the field. Your occupation is studies. And you require what is similar to the effort of the farmer to produce good results.

Knowing the essence of hard work is a part of quality education. A student who is lazy is obviously not learning enough. To be a hard-working student, you will have to be regular in class, attend talk shows, seminars and conferences if you get the opportunity. You also have to devise your own strategies of learning, search libraries, compare notes, do group discussions regularly, and join clubs in the school.

You need to get time to prepare for examinations as well. It is important to know the difference between learning and preparation for examination. Those who do not know the difference between the two commit many serious mistakes.

First of all, you are in school to acquire knowledge to make your life and society better, so you are in school to educate yourself. But learning happens in stages. And there are various levels of learning. One stage or level may lay the foundation for the other, and it continues in that order until you finally get what you need.

Examinations are intended to find out if the learning outcomes have been achieved. For example, the Basic Education Certificate Examination (BECE) is to find out whether the student has the correct foundation that would help them to carry out learning at the Senior High School. And the WASSCE is also to find out whether the student has what will enable them carry out learning at the tertiary level.

In this regard, past questions only serve to assist with the preparation for whatever exams one has to write. It is not needed in the knowledge acquisition process. Therefore, in your quest to work hard, avoid the habit of learning past questions. You solve past questions to have a feel of examination settings. It makes you know how you would have fared if you sat for that paper.

It is academically unhealthy to habitually study past questions. Since examinations normally lead to the award certificates, it is easy for students' attention to be shifted from acquiring education to acquiring certificates. But certificates cannot equip you with any problem-solving skill, or make you confident, comfortable and effective at the place of work.

Take, for instance, being trained as a doctor. The grades will give you the certificate and license to work at a hospital. But when you are at the consulting room and the patients start coming, the grade will not be needed; you will only need to apply what you studied.

Therefore, the best way to study is to study with the field of work or work place in mind, not the examination hall. You study as you imagine yourself at the work place. You study with a mental simulation of the real field environment. With this, you can imagine some of the possible challenges that may be faced. And with the teachers and friends around, you ask the right questions for assistance to help your training.

Another problem with past questions is that you do not need to understand the answers and the process of arriving at them. You only need to know and remember them. The mess here is that you end up with information without understanding. But you see, it is one thing to know that your name is say, Patrick, and it is completely another thing to understand why your name is Patrick. The real world or work place requires understanding. As a result, getting there through the study of past questions will make it extremely difficult to perform well at work.

You are not at the Senior High School to make grades to the university. No! You are there to prepare yourself or lay the foundation for university education. The grade you get is not that foundation. The knowledge and understanding, attitudes and habits you form are the foundation.

Your focus must be beyond your terminal exams or WASSCE. Learn because you need some knowledge to work with; learn because you want ideas to make your life and country better. When learning is done this way, you are able to make meaning from what you learn. This way of learning establishes a link between knowledge and needs. If what you know does not relate to your needs, it is no knowledge. It will not take the study of past questions to take Ghana to the moon or build a space station for Ghana.

You must think studies, sleep studies and dream studies. The last thing that puts you to sleep should be your thoughts about the important things you encountered in the day. Thomas Alva Edison said, 'None of my inventions came by accident, they came by hard work.' It is said that out of the twenty-four hours in the day, he was always at his laboratory working and experimenting. He slept for only five hours a day.

This is not to say you should sleep for five hours daily. It is just to suggest to you how those who succeeded made it; it is to give you an understanding of hard work. All those that have influenced the world positively worked very hard.

Make very good use of the siesta. Just lie on your bed and relax your body and brain. For those 30 minutes or so, try to think about nothing. The observance of the siesta is good for mental health and growth, so do not take it lightly. After the various lessons of the day, and your encounters with several teachers, the siesta relieves you of stress, helps cardiovascular functions, helps your memory and improves your alertness.

The time for the siesta is too short for deep sleep. It is not the best for teachers to come round before the siesta is observed. If for nothing at all, use that moment to learn how to keep quiet. Some people do not know how to keep quiet. They talk and talk and talk, even in their sleep. If you are that type, learn to sometimes keep quiet. Also, whenever you are tired, play some games, get yourself enough rest, and get back to work as soon as possible.

HONESTY

There is one way to find out if a man is honest: ask him; if he says yes, you know he's crooked.

Mark Twain

Aesop told a story of Mercury and the Woodman: A woodman was felling a tree on the bank of a river. Accidentally, his axe fell into the water, and immediately sank to the base of the river. In great distress, he sat by the side of the river and lamented bitterly. Mercury, who was the owner of the river, appeared, at that moment, before him.

Upon hearing the sad story of the Woodman, Mercury dived into the river and brought a golden axe.

'Is this your axe?' he asked.

'No,' replied the man.

He dived again and brought another one that was silver. The Woodman again said that was not his axe. He dived the third time and brought one that looked like that of the Woodman's.

When the woodman saw it, he exclaimed, 'That is mine!'

Mercury was so pleased with the man that he gifted the man both the silver and golden axes. It is hard to resist the temptation of gold and silver, but the Woodman was just honest.

An honest person does not lie, either in words or deeds. So honesty simply means being frank or truthful. Yes, there are times when telling the truth becomes a bit challenging. Your parents trust you so much that you feel they will be disappointed if they get to hear the truth. There is a time, when telling the truth may let you miss something you would dearly love. But tell it anyway and face the consequences.

Lies should be avoided, irrespective of how insignificant they may appear to be because any lie is a lie—whether black or white. And a conscience that can endure a little lie can do the same for a bigger lie. Besides, there is no difference between a small lie and a big lie. They do the same work and have the same effect: they make you dishonest, and scar your smooth conscience.

It is a disaster when telling lies becomes a culture. Many people see nothing wrong at all with lies. And the use of the mobile phones has compounded the problem. People, in their conversations on the phone, tell dizzying lies. The danger with lies is that it engenders mistrust. Nobody will trust a liar. But trust is needed in marriages, businesses and organizations. When they fail, they have a serious effect on a country.

Both at home and in school, you must be honest. Let your parents, teachers and colleagues see that you are honest. You must own up in school and at home for any mistake you commit. By doing so, you prepare yourself for a life of honesty, which will be of great value to your future life and the country as a whole. Stakeholders of organizations and company owners will always look for honest people to steer their affairs. Honest people are trusted with sensitive positions.

Do not be afraid to say, 'I am the one', 'I was wrong', 'I cannot do that', 'I do not have it', 'I cannot help you', 'I said it', etc. Dishonesty creates a lot of undue pressure for people as they have to commit a lot of evil in order to cover up themselves. Honesty will help make you a quality human resource.

MODESTY AND SELFLESSNESS

Modesty simply means moderation or simplicity in what one does. This is one of the greatest virtues you can give yourself as it makes you less selfish. Every human being is selfish so the good ones are those who are less selfish. Selfish people want everything for themselves.

This attitude can easily lead to extravagance. And extravagance and selfishness breed corruption. Another problem with this is that those who live this way struggle to adjust to hard times. As a result, they normally end up with depression and some even commit suicide. So modesty is very important. It will help reduce the pressure this selfish desire places on you.

It is not possible to get everything in life. But the life of extravagance pushes people to go almost for everything because they can afford them. Since there are ups and downs in life, the extravagant people, who are known for the ups alone, are not prepared for the downs. They just have no idea what it is to be in difficult times. This is ugly, they normally get depressed and commit suicide. Modesty puts you in a safe zone and prepares you for all seasons. People who are modest can adequately handle both good times and hard times.

HUMILITY

Ernest Hemingway said, 'There is nothing noble in being superior to your fellow man; true nobility is being superior to your former self.' Life is designed in a manner that things are always in their right proportions, such that anything less or more of itself constitutes a problem.

The lack of humility leads to an exaggeration of self-worth. And an exaggerated self is more than the true self and this constitutes an abnormality. This abnormality destroys the person himself and also creates a problem for those around.

This means that humility preserves those who have it, and it also does a lot of good to those who are nearby. Proud people have no love as they always see themselves to be better than others. The implication of this is that people who lack humility are ignorant since they have false knowledge of themselves.

The trait of humility is a special tool that needs to be fully utilized. And this is the appropriate stage to cultivate it if you do not have it. Humility will serve you very well wherever you find yourself.

In school, it attracts good friends, and wins you teachers' respect. It produces better students because with humility, one is not ashamed to say, 'I do not know'. You are not afraid or ashamed to ask questions that others may consider stupid. You do not and cannot know everything. No matter the level of knowledge one acquires, there is always something to learn.

And with knowledge, there is always someone around you or somewhere who knows what you do not know. There will be people who can do things you may not be able to do. In situations like this, you need to consult them and be ready to learn from them. The absence of humility will create a serious challenge for you. Your colleagues will find you obnoxious. And this can easily make you lonely.

It is good to be active in class and answer questions where necessary. But be measured in your approach. Do not rush to raise your hand to answer all questions even if you know them all. You need to give the opportunity for others to also answer some of the questions. If possible, wait until no one is able to answer before you raise your hand to answer. In group discussions, do not do all the talking. Give room for others to make their points.

Humility produces selflessness—a quality so vital for peace and prosperity. It makes you want for others what you want for yourself. Humility will always uplift you and give you a good name among people; it will always make you rational.

But it is important you do not mistake humility for sheepishness. To be humble is not to be making obeisance, and prostrating before friends and superiors. You do not have to always have your hands at your back and smile, or laugh unnecessarily in front of people when there is nothing to smile about. Do not have your head down when you stand before people. Stand straight and look into their eyes.

If you come from a rich home, count yourself fortunate. But those from poor homes must be treated with love and respect. The only difference is that they do not have the opportunity you have. You can learn from Kobina in 'For Whom Things Did Not Change', a short story from Ama Ata Aidoo's *No Sweetness Here.*

PLANNING AND DECISION MAKING SKILLS

Give me six hours to chop down a tree and I will spend the first four sharpening the axe.

Abraham Lincoln

Life is full of needs in one form or the other, and the ability to plan helps us meet many of these needs. Good planning readies and cushions you against unforeseen situations. Moreover, it is hard to make meaningful progress without planning. The reason is that nothing meaningful can be achieved by accident. Whatever comes to you on its own may go or disappear on its own. And whatever is gotten by planning, may by planning be maintained.

When actions are backed by good plans, there is efficient time use and quality outcome. The absence of plans will lead to things being done anyhow. And when things are done anyhow, any outcome is accepted. As a result, it is difficult to even measure progress made. Worse of all, there is no sense of direction.

The best time to cultivate a planning and decision-making habit is now. These skills will make you organized, prudent, help you use your time well and excel as a student, and prepare you for a successful adult life. It takes an organized person to plan.

The use of a diary matters a lot here. Unfortunately, the diary and its use are almost alien to many students. And it is quite understandable because they hardly see this practice around them. And the few who have what they call diaries only use them to write down sermons or notes at conferences or seminars. It is possible to have more than one diary book as parents and friends may gift you diaries at the beginning of the year. In such cases, there is nothing wrong in carrying one around as your notebook or pad.

Someone may borrow your notebook or pad to learn a thing or two, but your diary cannot be borrowed. In fact, it is personal and contains personal information. It contains your plans and resolutions, and these are not to be shared with others. If you misplace it, somebody who finds it may have access to the information in it. This is one reason it is advisable to have a notepad on you and keep your diary at home.

The use of diaries is not just an end in itself; it unconsciously builds several traits that are required for a successful academic life. First of all, it boosts memory. The diary itself is a long term memory material. For example, with your 2015 diary, you can easily remember any special experience you had in any of the months in that year. In the short term, the brain is more likely to recollect what you write down as compared to what is not written. So when you make an entry in your diary, it somehow gets memorized unconsciously.

It also inspires creativity. The entries made in the diary are not normally done the way notes are written. They are personalized. And because they are records of experiences, effort is made to write them in a manner that best represents the situation for you. Coming up with appropriate words, colours and images to do such a thing sharpen the creative ability. There are a lot of reflections in making diary entries. These reflections busy the imaginative part of the brain thereby making it sharp.

The diary may not be writing alone; it can be drawings or sketches, pictures or images. It could be a picture that day that reminds you of something special. You may write to describe the situation and insert the picture. If you can draw well, you may also make drawings of peculiar scenes and short notes to connect to them.

Further, it can improve your language and writing skills. As you learn to use appropriate words and language structures to write your experiences, you become better in the use of language and in writing as well.

Using a diary is not difficult at all. You may forget to write in your diary for some days since it is something you are beginning to do. But this will improve with time. A serious and meaningful life will present you with certain events and circumstances for which records will have to be taken. Within the 24 hours you spend in a day, something will either intrigue or bore you; something may make you happy or sad. And these are what you must write about.

The culture of using personal diaries helps students in countless ways. The absence of such a good habit will make you predisposed to negligence. It will weaken your ability to pay attention to details. It will work against the organization of your life and, by extension, your planning skills.

Let us explore the planning and decision-making skills. Planning is simply setting a goal and outlining how to achieve it. Planning could also be seen as the ordering of your decisions. A body of decisions together as a unit is a plan. It involves a goal, thought processes, some actions, and implementation. Since planning involves decision making, it is necessary to know how decisions are made.

The bedrock of a good decision is quality information or sound knowledge. To arrive at this, quality questions must be asked. And to understand what a quality question is, a good understanding of what an answer is matters. An answer is a response that satisfies a need or curiosity. Therefore, when a question attracts a response that adequately satisfies a curiosity, that question is termed a quality question. Series of such questions are needed in the decision making process.

In the process, the answers to some of the questions may raise further questions. This is what constitutes a *thought process.* And it goes on and on until there is enough information upon which a sound decision could be taken. Take, for example, a decision you want to make whether or not to have a 'boy/girlfriend'. The process may be something like this:

A) Why should I?

i)   To feel good and loved
- ✓ Is this the best way to feel good and loved?

ii)   To have someone I can spend time with
- ✓ Is this the best thing to do?
- ✓ Is this the best way to spend my time?

- ✓ Do I really need this?
- ✓ How will this help my studies?

iii) To experiment and enjoy sex

- ✓ Why should I do this?
- ✓ Do I really need this?
- ✓ Is this time the best?
- ✓ Are there possible dangers or risks?
- ✓ How will this help my studies?
- ✓ Will my parents be happy with this?
- ✓ What price will I pay should I do this? Do the benefits worth the price?

B) Why should I not?

i) To avoid early pregnancy

- ✓ What will early pregnancy cost me?
- ✓ What is wrong with early pregnancy?
- ✓ Is early pregnancy a problem?

ii) To avoid contracting any STI

- ✓ What will be the effect of an STI?
- ✓ Can't I use condom to protect myself?
- ✓ Are condoms reliable?

iii) Not to hurt my parents and family

- ✓ How can doing this hurt my parents and family?
- ✓ Is it not my right?

iv) To avoid waste of time

- ✓ In what way will this save me time?
- ✓ What could be the alternative activities for this time?

v) To stay focused on my studies

- ✓ How can this be a distraction?
- ✓ What will I be distracted from?
- ✓ Why do I need to stay focused?

In doing this, what will be the price to pay? Are the benefits worth the price?

From here, a decision is then taken based on the answers, and how satisfactory they are. This decision is then dated and written in your note or diary. For example:

20th January, 2018

Hmmm! It was really tough, but I took the decision not to have a boy/girlfriend until the age of 23. I am aware of what my friends will say and do; especially, Peter and Lois. But I am prepared for them.

So in your notebook or diary, you have this simple entry. From the above, you now know how you arrived at this decision. This decision is your goal. But that is not the end. You are left with what to do to ensure that it is done. And another thought process is needed to decide on the actions to be taken to achieve that objective. The final thing is the implementation. You do not just get up and say, 'I will not have a boy or girlfriend until I turn 23'. After backing this decision with a good action plan, you stick to it, and take responsibility for it.

There are always specific things to do in order to get whatever you want. As a result, plan your day with specific tasks, and discipline yourself to keep and follow them. Every good student is a good planner. As a business person sits back and checks their sales at the end of every working day, good students will also have to check their list of activities to see what they did well, and what should be improved upon. Those who are not used to planning will struggle with it initially, but with practice, there will be improvement.

PART V

DISTRACTORS

One of the hardest things to do is to concentrate or stay focused for a long period of time. There are many things within and around individuals that distract a lot. Normally, the things that are very beneficial appear difficult to be done. But the ones that are less beneficial get done easily. There is always a great tendency for attention to be shifted to things that do not require much effort. Therefore, in any field of endeavour, there are things one needs to ward off in order to stay focused.

The current era, though full of great opportunities, has a threatening downside. Just as it presents numerous opportunities for human excellence, it equally presents serious destructive challenges. In addition to this, the adolescent age is the most slippery stage of human development and presents students with some of the most dreadful distractors that can ever be imagined. We take a look at a few of them.

SEX AND AMOROUS FEELING

Shirley Feldman, a psychologist at Stanford University said, 'Sexual arousal emerges as a new phenomenon in adolescence and it is important to view sexuality as a normal aspect of adolescent development.' There are a lot of challenges with sex because of its nature and, largely, the misconceptions about it. This becomes even worse for adolescents as they do not have the developed thinking capacity to rightly scrutinize the issues of sex for themselves.

The growing teenagers are faced with many issues of sex that they virtually know nothing about. This ignorance, coupled with the misinformation they receive from the media and peers, lead them into committing life-threatening mistakes. Therefore, much education is needed to rightly position them to handle sex and sexual arousals in ways that will not destroy their lives.

As Shirley intimates, sexual arousal is a powerful new experience that adolescents go through. Some boys, at this stage, experience regular erections. Sometimes, many of these erections will not be because they are thinking about sex, but the changes in their bodies and other hormonal products may cause that. Occasionally, some may have wet dreams. Girls, at this stage, may also have vaginal discharges as a result of either thinking about sex or hormonal changes in the body.

At this point, some people may resort to doing certain things to satisfy their sexual urges. A few will even go to the extent of experimenting with it. Some engage in sex due to curiosity and others from peer influence. They try to hide these things from their parents, and this does a lot of harm.

It is instructive to note that sexual arousal or the urge for sex is a vital component of the human makeup. As the human body is designed for food, and there are organs specifically designed to handle that, so is the human body designed for sex and organs equally designed for that. So sex is good, just as food is.

But just as people do not eat any kind of food at all or eat at odd times because the human body is designed for food, similarly, people should not engage in sex with anybody or anything at any time at all just because the body is designed for sex. Things must be done the way they are meant to be done and not the way they are thought to be done.

To be able to manage the issues of sex (sexual intercourse) very well, emotional literacy is needed. There is the need to go beyond the feeling that comes with sex and explore the significance or purpose of it. This makes understanding the very first step towards the proper handling of sex and sexual arousals important.

First, it is normal to have the urge for sex as an adolescent. You are not a bad boy or girl when you have that experience. It is a very good sign that you are developing normally. Those who do not have that urge must notify their parents. It will have to be medically investigated earlier as it may be the sign of a biological problem.

The sexual urges can be very powerful or strong. Like any other emotion, the best way to handle it is to not suppress it. Any attempt to suppress an emotion may, most likely, lead to depression. In this case, since sexual arousal starts in the mind, it is in the mind that any positive attempt can be made to handle it. This is where emotional literacy comes in. But it must be known that when people are exposed to any sexual material, almost no amount of emotional literacy can offer any help.

It is not wise to consciously create problems for ourselves and then waste time to solve them. What this means is that there must be breaks on the things that will elicit sexual arousal. But unfortunately, the nature of the era, and the state of the country and world provide exposure to sex at a very early age. You are surrounded by a lot of things that arouse this urge for sex. The TV stations, radio stations, the celebrities, the internet, are all whipping your desire for sex almost on a daily basis.

As a result of this, it has been thought that what can be done to help you is to teach you how to engage in safe sex. But at this stage of your life, there is nothing like safe sex for you. You can be protected against STIs and early pregnancies, but you cannot be protected against the wild and complicated emotions that come with sex. You do not have the capacity to handle these complicated emotions that come with sex. No provision for safe sex was made for you at this stage because this stage is not meant for sex. There is only one thing to know and understand about sex: **This stage is not meant for sex**.

One of the things about sex is that it is not for fun. It satisfies a need, and fortunately, you do not have that need now. There is great pleasure in sex, but that is not the purpose of sex. It is just for the motivation to have sex. With the inherent nature of humans bent on doing what is always against nature, it takes such a mysterious pleasure to make people voluntarily have sex.

Sex was designed to ensure continuity of human life on earth. Apart from this, it also renders some other services to the body, and that will be discussed later. So sex is not the feeling of pleasure. It is the action of intercourse and its effect, not the pleasure. The feeling of pleasure people get during sex is not the act itself, but a bait to have sex. In this way, when people go in for the pleasure, they end up carrying out the creator's design just like bees do to flowers in their search for nectar.

A simple definition of sex will be an activity that makes a man and a woman one through the exchange of body fluids, with the resultant effect of bonding and an attempt to produce species of their own kind. Therefore, sex is for two primary things: bonding and reproduction. The one with the most serious upshot is the bonding. Bonding here means becoming one with the person with whom one engages in sex. And this is the source of the emotional complications that come with sex.

Common observation reveals the change in behaviour and attitudes of boys and girls after their first experience of sex. It should be interesting to know what causes that. But obviously, it is the sex experience that is responsible for that. The deficit in behavioural and attitudinal propriety alone should be enough reason to discourage adolescents from engaging in premature sex.

Also, those who engage in early sex end up developing a greater urge for sex. Such an attitude will make boys devalue girls. And girls, on the other hand, will be seen as sexual objects. The emotional problems associated with sex, in many cases, prevent people from reaching their full potentials. Apart from some girls having to face some life-threatening conditions as a result of early sex, it wastes a lot of precious time.

Understanding the concept of sex will help you handle it well. As you grow, this urge for sex will keep coming. What must be done is the effort to control or manage it. When you get this feeling for the opposite sex, it is not an invitation for sex, but just to remind you that you are growing well and healthy. It also reminds you of the responsibilities ahead of you, for which you have to improve your way of doing things. You can use this emotion positively by making it remind you of your dreams. You also need to reduce your sexual fantasies. As much as possible, you must stay away from pornographic materials. Withdraw from friends who frequently discuss sex and sexual materials.

Your parents love you so much that they will not refuse you any good thing if they can afford it. So why will they not permit you to indulge in sex now? Is it because they want to starve you of sex? If sex is good for you at this time of your life, they would have provided you a sexual partner. But this is not the case because every parent wants to see their ward succeed in life. And sex, at this stage, is a threat to your success in school.

At this stage of your life, one of the greatest mistakes you will ever make is to indulge in sex. If you have already indulged in that, admit it as a mistake that you have made. After all, everybody makes mistakes. The way forward is to seek help or counselling. Be courageous and inform your parents, talk it out with them and let them help you.

If you are not able to control yourself and you engage in the act of sex, the best thing to do is to tell your parents. The solution to this problem lies in telling your parents and not friends. It will not only hurt you if you hide it from them, it will get worse. Your parents will not kill you; they will rather help set you free and bring you back on track. Sometimes some parents, by their nature, make it difficult for mistakes like this to be made known to them. In this case, you could channel it through a trusted relative or friend of your parents.

Learn to develop healthy relationship or friendship with the opposite sex. Girls are different from boys, and boys are also different from girls. In view of this, it is important to have friends who are of the opposite sex. Their special abilities will complement yours. You can also learn very important lessons that will be useful in your future marriage and occupational life.

There are some girls who fear or do not like the company of boys; and the same applies to some boys. This is a problem because the two sexes have unique qualities. Take advantage of the opportunity to learn how to associate with the opposite sex. It is said that Nicola Tesla had a very poor social life despite his scientific success. This is because he was only concerned with his scientific studies. He was always at the laboratory and so perhaps he knew how to relate with laboratory apparatus more than he knew to relate with fellow human beings. And that was a disaster!

You will, by all means, marry, and even if you do not marry, you will have the opposite sex at your place of work where you will have to work as a team. This friendship is even important in your academic endeavour. Learn to eat, play and think together with the opposite sex without any urge for sex. It is very exciting to play with the opposite sex. Try it and you will love it. Take advantage of this unique relationship and grow into a responsible adult.

THE LURE OF MONEY

It is good to have money and all the things that money can buy, but it is good, too, to check up once in a while to make sure that you haven't lost the things that money cannot buy.

George Lorimer

There is arguably nothing in the world that may worry, enslave, and make people more miserable than poverty. It is never a normal or good thing to be poor. The consequences of poverty are dire. And the worse of it is that it breeds poor thinking. Therefore, great effort must be made to ensure that people get out of it. And, in fact, this is one of the reasons quality education is needed. It is quality education that would get you out of poverty. And frankly, anything that interrupts or interferes with your education serves to draw you close to it (poverty).

Some of these interruptions come in the guise of money. There are money-making openings that are a threat academic excellence. Sports bets are paramount among these. The law states that people above 18 years of age can engage in it. But it is very unhealthy for students, especially you.

Money is attractive, and just like any other attractive thing, the moment you get a little of it, there is the temptation to push for more. The result of this is that one ends up getting addicted to the source of that money. But the challenge is that nothing steals time more than an addiction. What happens then is that the time to be spent to educate yourself or learn a trade or skill will largely be spent on the bets. This will obviously lead to low academic performance or poor acquisition of skills.

Another danger of these quick money-making ventures is that they make people more money conscious than work conscious. They produce a very poor orientation towards money. And this state is very terrible as people who have poor orientation of money are a serious threat to life—the very thing education is intended to improve.

It is important to know the link between work and money. This can best be illustrated by the process of photosynthesis in plants. In doing this, plants produce their own food, glucose; and release oxygen in the process. But the substance of their activity to them (the plants) is glucose and not oxygen per se. Similarly, the work that people do is aimed at solving individual or societal problems and they end up getting rewarded for the problem they solve.

Work is aimed at rendering services to people who are in need of them. People can stop making money, but they cannot and must not stop working because services are always needed. So when people value money over work, there will serious problems in society.

In some places, there are a few students who take care of themselves in school because they have no parents or guardian to help them. Almost all such people resort to gambling and these bets to cater for themselves and their academic needs. This is an unfortunate situation since such activities will by all means affect their performance in school.

It is not wise for those who do not face similar challenge to engage in that just for youthful escapade. Once there are people to take care of your financial needs, what remains your occupation is learning.

THE ABUSE OF TECHNOLOGY

Technology is the fulcrum of modernization. The learning opportunities it makes available to students are almost limitless. There is, therefore, no way students are to be discouraged from the use of technology. It can really contribute greatly to students' academic success.

But almost everything that has ever been made to solve a problem has come with its own problems, and technology is not an exception. Even many mature adults struggle to overcome some of the negative effects of technology. What then can the situation be for adolescents? For them, the challenge is overwhelming.

When studied carefully, it will be observed that when people have their smart phones on them, they hardly stay for about five minutes without touching or using them. Perhaps the only time an adolescent at home who has a smart phone may not be using it in their leisure time is when they are asleep or have their batteries down. This suggests the addictive nature of technology.

But the quest for quality education requires that students stay very well organized and have their own schedules for various activities. You are to have your priorities right and resist the temptation to spend time on what has not been planned for.

Technology, by its nature, has all the attraction and power to lure anyone to what is not planned for. It is not a mere coincidence that technology giants including Bill Gates and Steve Jobs controlled and limited their children's access to social media, computer games and the internet. It is even said that Steve Jobs denied his children access to the iPhone that he himself helped develop.

These were done to protect the children and to help them steer from distractors. If you are the kind who does not have parents that can help you that way, help yourself. With the smart phone, you do not need to come out of your room and gad about before it is seen that you are roaming. You can be in you room and roam around the world the whole day provided there is enough data, and your battery is powerful enough.

There is need for great discipline to stay focused, and avoid the distractions that come with technology. Choose, rather, the side of technology that will make you a successful student.

PART VI

THE ESSENCE OF EDUCATION

Education is what took the world out of the Dark Ages. It is the reason human beings don't travel long distances on foot any longer. It is the reason some people don't sweep with brooms and farm with cutlasses and hoes anymore. It is the reason Europe, America and some parts of Asia are free from malaria. It is the reason we don't trade with cowries anymore. And it is the reason for civilization around the world.

Education is not just to offer facility with numeracy and literacy, but refine humans for a refined world. As the refinery does to minerals, school does the same for humans. What this means is that people go to school to get themselves 'processed'. And this is the reason there are dos and don'ts in schools.

These rules and regulations are not to temper with the rights of students or limit their freedom to explore but intended to mould them into a certain desired shape—one that would be in their own interest and in the interest of society.

So education, apart from equipping people with skills, provides knowledge that leads to the improvement of attitudes and behaviour. Therefore, the certification for education is the demonstration of knowledge by way of competence at work, and display of refined attitudes and behaviour; not just the possession of paper certificates. Sadly, the premium placed on the award of certificates makes people see the certificates as the end of schooling.

THE LINK BETWEEN EDUCATION AND EXAMINATIONS

Can there be learning without any form of examination? Whether people learn on our own or under someone's tutelage, there will always be the need for examination in one way or the other. This will be needed to help find out whether there is progress in what the person is learning or not. It is important for students to understand the purpose of examination as it forms part of the learning process.

Since there are various bodies of knowledge one can acquire, there are equally different forms of examinations. Those who learn practical skills carry out practical examination. But the most common to students is the academic examination.

The challenge with the type of examination common to you is that in writing them, you are not allowed to open to or refer to any book or material. Because of this, it is easily mistaken for a test of memory instead of learning. But it becomes a huge problem if the whole learning process is given a memory test instead of a learning test.

One of the disadvantages of this kind of examination is that it leads to various forms of malpractices as those who struggle with memory may engage in many unlawful and inappropriate ways to pass. But examination malpractices defeat the purpose of education. The bad news is that where examination malpractice is rife, there is little or no education.

The examination scenario can best be compared to a hospital. There is no patient who goes to a hospital to deceive doctors or medical practitioners. As the doctor needs the patient's cooperation to help heal them, so does the school need the student's cooperation to get them refined and acquire needed skills.

What the patient does after the medication or treatment enables the doctor to assess their rate or level of recovery. It is unimaginable for patients to pretend to doctors that they are well when they are really suffering. Anyone who does that qualifies for a mental examination.

And examination malpractice is not far from this. As the doctor depends on the activities and responses of the patients to assess their recovery, so is examination intended to assess learners' progress.

It is a fact that a student who knows much will not cheat in an examination. Therefore, when students resort to foreign materials, it means they do not know enough. But if people do not yet know what they desire to know, what must they do? Obviously, they must continue to learn until they know enough. So examination malpractice is self-deception. And worse of it all, it is the strongest foundation for corruption in students.

However, while examination malpractices must be discouraged, it is equally important to consider the enormous pressure on some students to engage in that. This may provide some clues to addressing it. It has already been established that we cannot live without examination; unless we are not ready to learn anything new.

Frankly, one of the hardest things to do is to take or write a formal examination. It almost always comes with pressure no matter the form it takes, and no matter how prepared the individual is. The reason is that no one wants to write an examination and fail. And the notion and possibility of failure is so dreadful that everybody will do all it takes to avoid that. Nobody wants to fail, no parents want their children to fail, and no school wants their students to fail, so the pressure is huge.

There are exceptional cases where people fail examinations because of their poor attitudes and behaviour. But quite apart from that, it must be understood that failure is part of the learning process. There is nothing wrong for students to do what they know, under the circumstance, and yet fail examination. It is normal and sometimes very important. In fact, it is normal to fail an examination.

At a point in Albert Einstein's life, he sat for an entrance examination and passed mathematics and physics but failed French, chemistry and biology. And that was not the end; he failed again some other times later on. Along the line, some students may never fail an examination, but that is not the benchmark of an excellent student.

The meaning of failure is that 'it cannot be done this way'. This is why failure is a lesson. It is a great lesson to know that something ought not to be done a certain way. Such a lesson will then initiate the steps to find out how it ought to be done. So failure in an examination or anything must not be a dreaded end; rather, a painful means for further inquiry and realignment of thoughts, and a possible change of direction.

GETTING READY FOR EXAMINATIONS

Like any other business or activity people do, certain elements should be considered in order to do well in examinations. Motivation is central to excelling in examinations. Your motivation must be very high. The level of knowledge you have acquired should motivate you. This means if you have not learnt enough, you need to speed up and cover enough; the absence of that will discourage you.

Also, you must believe in yourself and have a strong desire to pass. It is good to remember that first of all, people have written similar exams and passed so if you do what they did, you can also pass as they passed. In addition, those going to write the exams are just like you; so you have every reason to believe in yourself. And the goal or future you have set for yourself should motivate you to do your best in the exams.

With your motivation very high, and a good dose of self-confidence, you can then plan and prepare for the exams. Group studies are very important, so aside from your individual studies, get a study group. This could be a minimum of three and a maximum of five. Even if you are a day student, you could form a group with students in the neighbourhood. These students should not necessarily be students from your school. You must make schedules for your individual and group studies. The plan should help you decide what you must do and what you must avoid.

However, you must avoid over-learning as that will wear you down, especially getting to the final days of the examination. You need to be in the best frame of mind anytime you are studying or about writing a paper. But over-learning will work against your brain and reduce your output. Therefore, get enough rest or sleep if you get tired.

Finally, manage the expectations from people. Parents, family members, the school and friends may expect a lot from you, but be yourself. Manage their expectations, and do not let their expectations pile undue pressure on you. Also, avoid competition with and from peers. You are not in any race or a contest with anyone. Enter the examination hall with confidence and well composed, waiting for whatever questions they may bring your way.

THE HARVEST OF EDUCATION

'We had a huge task when we first started in 1960. At that time, our population was 1.6 million, out of that 1.3 million lived in squatters—not counting thousands of others living in slum areas and old buildings,' said Lui Thai Ker, the architect credited with the design of modern Singapore, about Singapore's early days.

The same can be said of Hong Kong, Japan and all advanced countries we have in the world today. What we see from these countries now are the harvests of their education. They were built with the education of their people.

The Dutch say, 'God created the world, but the Dutch created the Netherlands.' If the Dutch built The Netherlands, Ghanaians will have to build Ghana. There must be the hope for a country that everyone can be proud of. And that is hoped to be the harvest the country will reap from the education of her students. To achieve this, the following are paramount.

SOUND SPIRITUALITY

It is said that one day, the boarders in one of the secondary schools in the country refused to eat the meal served them because they had information from the president of one of the religious groups in the school that the food had been spiritually turned into maggots. And you can imagine the mess this situation created. In fact, there are records of similar or different instances in many other schools.

Beyond the borders of the schools, the country is replete with very troubling issues that arise from religion. These issues, if not resolved, would continue to work against our progress as individuals and as a country. Our most reliable tool for the redress of this challenge is quality education. Therefore, getting a good picture of religion may offer some guide to this end. Religion has many adherents, making it a very special area. Because it is linked to the supernatural, it comes with extreme reverence and fear. And this has several ramifications.

If an instruction is said to have come from a supernatural source, the natural response (from the religious) is that they would not dare question it even if it does not sound right because to do so, is to question the authority of the supernatural and that is sacrilegious. This makes the patronage of spirituality, though important, the most effective tool for scoundrels to exploit or take advantage of people who are religious. It has the potential to reduce the gains of education to zero as it hardly encourages sound thinking.

For example, it is very easy for many people who are religious to attribute almost any accident to evil spirits. The problem with this kind of thinking is that people end up in the situation where, instead of properly thinking through the causes of a problem to come up with lasting solution, they rather look up to or depend on spirits to help address it. Nothing could be as pathetic as this.

There is no attempt to refuse the existence of spiritual influences. And actually, spiritual influences are real everywhere in the world. They only manifest differently in different locations or places. Even in advanced countries, they are there. But the way they are approached in our country leaves much to be desired. Though it is very dangerous to downplay spiritual things, it is more dangerous to spiritualize everything. That, in itself, is pure ignorance. Moreover, spirituality is not against common sense. You can think right and still be spiritual.

It is important to develop way beyond the ignorance associated with religion since it draws people back and creates a lot of problems for society. There are evil spirits in Europe, but why is it that they do not 'cause' many road accidents as they do in Africa? The money-making rituals seen on many of our local television stations seem to create the impression that rituals can make people rich. But if rituals are not needed to make millionaires in America and Europe, then they are not needed to make millionaires in Ghana or Africa.

Again, whereas soil fertility and other best farming practices will lead to a bumper harvest, the religious people will say a god or some gods are responsible and so have to offer sacrifices to thank them. As the non-religious ones will be working around the clock to find ways to improve their lives, the religious will either be talking to their god or waiting for their god or gods to bring them solution. This is quite ravaging—it sucks!

There are cases of some students who spend a lot of their time doing what they call prayer instead of studying. Even when they have examination to write, they 'pray' more than they learn. Again, there is nothing against prayer. And, in fact, the one who does not pray or know how to pray is miserable, especially as an African. So, genuine prayer is very important.

The emphasis is genuine prayer, and this is what is recommended for you. It is not the type that enslaves or puts people into bondage. Neither is it the one full of ordinary noise where people return more dead than they went. Sadly, this type of genuine prayer is scarce in our country.

A survey shows that Africa is the most religious continent. If our kind of religion does any good, how can the section of the world that practices it most, be considered the darkest continent? And Africa is not only the poorest; it is arguably the most corrupt. It should not take any hard thinking to know that something is wrong with our form of spirituality. It is obvious our kind of spirituality has not improved our country and continent much if any.

In addressing the issue at stake, it is important to draw the difference between being religious and believing in the creator of the universe. Our kind of spirituality has so many red flags to be associated with this majestic Being. It is important to note that many of the things you see in our country and Africa, in general, as the worship of God have no relationship at all with the creator of the world. Nature reveals a very wonderful and smart God—a sound-thinking Being. But many of the practices we see around us are very ugly and extremely senseless to have a link with such a sound-thinking being. Unfortunately, since believing in the Creator is a spiritual exercise, He (The Creator) gets roped into all the mess associated with religion and spirituality.

Because of these many negative sides, spiritual issues have, for a long time, been seen as contrary to rational thinking or sound education. But this is very unfortunate. Since education has to do with the whole human being, spirituality cannot be seen as an opposing end of education because it (spirituality) is a component of humankind. Spirituality is what accounts for our superior thinking as human beings. It is what accounts for the endlessness of human life. So, in the absence of that, humans are not different from animals.

In fact, all forms of formal education are lower forms of spirituality since spirituality is nothing but superior knowledge. Therefore, spirituality and quality education are in perfect harmony. Perhaps the point of divergence is the concept of God. And this, in itself, is only misunderstanding of a term. Otherwise, there should be no problem at all. Those who are not comfortable with the term God, may choose whatever term they are comfortable with, and that will make no difference.

It only becomes a huge problem when the thought is entertained that there is no God. Not only is this the weirdest, it is the most reckless stance to take. As huge as the universe is, it is humanly impossible to gather enough evidence to conclusively say that there is no God. Truly, there are tough questions to ask about the existence of God, but there are tougher questions for the opposite. In chemistry, there is what is called balancing of chemical equations. Take God out and the equation of life can never be balanced.

He is the supreme intelligence behind all creation. He is the reason all planets stay in their orbits. He is the reason a male goat does not cross a male goat but a female goat. He is the reason the male sexual organ is different from the female sexual organ. He is the reason why even Siamese twins show some individuality. When he is taken out, what is expected is chaos. The next time you see orderliness, you have seen a part of the Creator.

Science explains that all of matter is attracted to one another by the force of gravity. This requires that there be a specific amount of matter in the universe, as a little more or a little less of it will destroy the universe. If it is a little less, the rate of contraction will be very fast, and the universe will collapse; if it is more, the rate of expansion will be faster. So, either way will destroy all creation.

The next is the amazing precision of the strong nuclear force between the neutrons and protons of elements. If this nuclear force is a little weak, almost all the other elements in the periodic table apart from hydrogen will not be formed—there would not be life in the first place. On the other hand, if it is a bit stronger above the normal, there will be serious radioactivity which will destroy all forms of life.

What probably qualifies to be the most amazing is our Earth itself and where it is located. There are other galaxies apart from the Milky Way. The nature of the other galaxies is such that human life cannot exist on them apart from the Milky Way galaxy, where our Earth is located. And even with the Milky Way Galaxy, the positions of the stars are such that there are not several but only one spot which can support life and that is exactly where our Earth is located.

The position of the Earth to the nearest star (the Sun) is such that if the Earth is a little closer than normal, we would burn to death, and if it is farther away than normal, we would freeze to death. To sustain life, the distance between the Sun and the Earth has to be carefully measured. If these signs are even not convincing enough, who ensured that precision, or did the measurement? The correct answer is key. However, you are free to give any answer that may suit what you believe.

It is very hard to suppose that there is no one behind this extreme intelligence and design. R. C. Sprawl said, 'It takes more faith to believe there is no God, than to believe there is God.' In fact, looking at the place of God in life, if even

He does not exist, we must invent Him. And that the greatest of all human inventions would be our invention of God.

Though there can be no one as miserable as the person who believes there is no God or Creator, such a one is better than a religious person. On many occasions, those who are atheists are intellectually and behaviourally better than many of the so-called religious people. And this is why our religiosity is a very challenging one.

In the history of mankind, religious people have caused more pain and sorrow, perhaps, than any other groups of people. The Supreme Being, who made all things, is one with what he has made. This is why he is called a father. Otherwise, how could a sexless being be called a father? But religion hardly teaches that. Religion creates a monster so that people could live in fear.

Spirituality is superior knowledge. So if our kind of spirituality is sound, our country should be one of the most advanced, looking at how religious we are. The contrast in the state of our country and continent should be enough to trigger a rethink of religion or our kind of spirituality.

The advice is not to quit your religion. But if God can be found there, find him and ignore the rituals. Find the sound spirituality in the religion you belong to, and if possible, throw the religious aspect away. Religion is that aspect that makes people enslaved, and makes people take advantage of their fellow human beings in the name of God. It is that aspect that puts fear into man not to question anything believed to have come from God.

But anything contrary to sound thinking cannot be of God. If God does not want the mind to be used, why would he create it? Spiritual things are not jokes; they are real indeed. Human beings are neither body nor spirit alone but a perfect combination of the two.

Like the order and design in the universe, there must be uniformity in the way issues are handled as far as the physical and spiritual are concerned. A disproportion between the physical and the spiritual will definitely cause a problem. Those who lean too much towards the physical will have their peculiar challenges and vice-versa. A balanced approach will be of much good to you and the country as a whole.

Such a balanced posture will position you for sound learning and give you the education needed to contribute your quota to the world before you depart from this world. Consult your parents and depend on them for sound spirituality if possible. If you have spiritual leaders, ask them good questions. Finally, pray when you have to pray, and study when you have to study. When you use your time to learn for 'prayers,' you are out of order; hence, committing an offence against the Creator. God can and will guide you, but will never do for you what you must do for yourself. This is sound spirituality.

PATRIOTISM

When people have great love for their country, they willingly serve and sacrifice their time and effort for her. Patriotism makes people do great things for their countries. The lifeline of prosperous countries is patriotism. With a country of various regions and ethnic groups, the greatest act of patriotism is to be nationalistic and not tribalistic. If individuals go along tribal lines, it will create a huge problem as that will make the country dangerously divided. The strength and prosperity of a country lie in the unity of her citizens.

Therefore, all tribal lines have to be erased to make room for a great country. Instead of saying, 'I am proud to be an Nzema, a Ga, etc.', it is much appropriate to say, 'I am proud to be a Ghanaian'. After all, of what use or good is it to be a 'proud' Nzema or Ashanti in a poor or backward Ghana? No single tribe can prosper above the prosperity of the country. The collective prosperity of all tribes is the prosperity of the country. It is said that the strength of a chain lies in its weakest link.

It is sound, therefore, to remember that because we are a country, the weakness of any single tribe is the weakness of the whole country just as a boil on your toe will affect your head. So there is no sense at all in living along tribal lines. Every Ghanaian student, irrespective of the language they speak, is a fellow citizen and must be treated with equal respect.

The country must be put first in the things you do. That is the best way a better country can be built for everyone to enjoy living in. Anything national must be of great value, particularly the constitution and the national flag. The constitution is the spirit, and the flag is the symbol of the country. What feeling would it evoke if there is small embroidery of the national flag in the top of the uniform of every Ghanaian student?

There are many instances where many people display ignorance of the significance of the national constitution and flag. Some people, for example, may decorate their houses or cars with foreign flags. It is a serious thing that ought not to be so. No matter the behaviour or state of one's parents, somebody else's cannot be yours. There is no option but to own them. In future, if you go to any advanced country and find even one of their citizens with the Ghana flag in their car or house, come back and do the same here. If it is hard for them to do that, it should equally be hard for us to do same.

Elsewhere, some people even salute their national flags as a sign of respect and love for country. Something similar or better should be done for our country. One of the best areas for mock rehearsal of patriotism and nationalism is your school. You have to use your school to practice how to be patriotic. You learn to sing your school anthem with passion, take good care of school property and not be comfortable to see anything that belongs to your school left in ruin. You obey school rules and regulations, etc. This way, you will find it easy to do same for the country when you are out of school.

And finally, you must have the mind-set of receiving education to contribute to the country, and not to get your share of what the country has. It is true that you have a right to what belongs to the country, but the mind-set of getting yourself educated in order to get your share of what is in the country will corrupt your education. And in fact, you do not need education to scramble for your share of what the country has.

This is a disastrous mind-set because it makes people inclined to looking for rewards instead of rendering services. It will turn society upside down and corrupt almost all morals. When what consumes people are rewards and money, it will be difficult to progress as a country. This will naturally make them tilt towards places where the rewards are easy to find. Another danger with this is that it becomes a loophole for foreign countries to exploit.

It will be used to sieve the best people (the most talented, physically strong and academically sharp) out of the country to develop their countries as ours remains undeveloped. Remember that the greatest resource of any country is its citizens (human resource) and not the natural resources. The cause of our underdevelopment is our lack of quality human resource and no other thing. You would not want to spend your productive years serving and building foreign countries, and then come home and die or die there and be brought home for a burial, would you?

RESPECT FOR THE ELDERLY

There are national cultures and out of these, countries create their national identities. All countries have their own cherished values. Some are given to food, some to drinks, some to work, some to ethics, some to sex, some to education, and others to immorality.

Our country is not an exception; we have ours. Though not all our practices are good, especially our religiosity. But there are some that are near perfect and must be cherished. Among these is our respect for the elderly. Respect is courtesy. It is how you speak or relate to someone to show whether or not they are worth your time, love, or attention as a result of your frame of mind towards them.

In this regard, your frame of mind towards the elderly must be that of high esteem. The way people relate or treat others depends on how they value or see them. So in order to respect the elderly, you must see them as they are: very important people. We are here because they brought us up. They are our foundation, so to disrespect them is to disrespect our foundation.

The elderly you meet might not be your direct relative, but are surely someone else's. They might not mean a lot to you, but they mean a lot to someone so you cannot disrespect them. Remember that any honour done the elderly is one to the country. Elsewhere, there is no difference between the young and the elderly. But for us, there was, there is and there will be.

In spite of what you learn from your much readings and studies, any elderly person knows several things that you do not and may never know. The respect for the elderly forms a very important part of our social structure, and must not be tampered with. There are so many things that must be learnt from the elderly, especially their experiences and wisdom.

If for nothing at all, they were born before we were born, so they deserve that respect. We believe in the blessings of the elderly; call it superstition. We believe the good things they say about us can bless us. It is not a myth, though science does not support it. Though some elderly may not conduct themselves as such, that does not give you the right to disrespect them. Just be who you must be, and let them be who they are.

However, the respect for the elderly must not be mistaken for backward behaviour. For example, it is not disrespectful to ask the elderly questions about what you do not understand. It is not disrespectful to let the elderly know that you have an opinion about something. It is not disrespectful to show individuality in your thinking.

DECENCY IN SPEECH

Language, as a means of communication, is intended to enhance social life. But just as language can be used to improve society, it can equally be used to foment trouble and destroy society. This presents us with the situation to decide which side to go.

Our constitution allows for freedom of speech. However, if this freedom ends up destroying us, then it is no freedom, but rather destruction in disguise. Without question, free speech is freedom indeed. We just must not use it to destroy ourselves.

Every human being wants to be respected and not be insulted. When people are disrespected, they get hurt and feel offended. The misuse of free speech is bound to produce so many unhealthy happenings in society. It is for this reason that effort must be made to desist from foul languages.

The Ghanaian has been one with decent language. This can be seen in the numerous proverbs and euphemisms we have in our local languages. They make things that are found to be offensive to be couched in language structures that make them less offensive.

But some foreign elements have crept in, and they are fast eroding this enviable aspect of the Ghanaian identity. Many people speak or use language with reckless abandon. Many radio stations and media outlets are rife with insults and inflammatory comments.

This situation is even worse among students. There have been several instances of students recording themselves using foul language and posting them on social media. The enthusiasm and excitements with which they do such things indicate how poorly some students are educating themselves. Civility of speech is a sign of a cultivated mind. You cannot afford to miss that mark.

DECENCY IN DRESSING

The good book says no one lights a candle and puts it under a bushel. So obviously, no one would spend a lot of money on expensive creams to get an improved skin only to cover it up with cassock-like apparels. Anyone with very nice body shape would want to use that as their currency and so may not want to put on anything that would devalue their currency. No one would spend huge amount of money on cosmetic surgeries only to cover them up from the public.

So there are various reasons people dress the way they dress or wear what they wear. Generally, dresses are made to provide warmth, comfort, confidence, and elegance. And these are basic human needs. But the extreme of them is counterproductive. This confirms the saying that, 'Too much of everything is bad.'

It is for this reason that the Ghanaian culture of modesty in dressing should not be traded for anything. And in fact, modesty would not rob anyone any of the benefits above. For example, confidence and elegance can be met in modesty.

Dressing forms part of body language so it is important you do not miscommunicate with yours. There are many ways some students (both boys and girls) dress these days that have to be re-examined. The truth is that when people put on mini dresses or provocative dresses, they just want to expose themselves in a measured or controlled way for a desired objective. In other words, there are parts of their bodies that they want people to see but there is a limit to what they want seen. Some men also dress in ways that raise questions. For some time now, the manner of dressing on many of the university campuses in the country has become a huge debate. Whereas everyone has the right to dress however they like, quality education would always make for propriety of appearance. You will never lose anything if you subscribe to decent dressing. And in fact, that is our culture.

Every occupation has its dress code; even delinquency has its dress code. So obviously, students (scholars in the making) should have a dress code. After all your education, you will still be a Ghanaian so learn to dress like an educated Ghanaian.

OUR TOMORROW TODAY

As a country, we must have our own way of doing things. There must be a time that a foreigner may love to do things the *Ghanaian way*—one of dignity and respect. Obviously, we have a long way to go in this regard, but it is attainable. The attitude of our students today will give a picture of the kind of tomorrow that awaits us as a country. For a promising tomorrow, the attitude of our students towards education must be exceptional.

There are mounting challenges, but they are surmountable. With enough determination, great love for country, and the resolve to build an enviable country, almost all challenges shall pale into nothingness. You are one of the country's greatest assets. Your inability to reach your highest potential will be a great disadvantage to your family and the country.

You may be a very good student. But remember you can still do better than you are doing. You have a very elastic potential, so stretch it as much as possible and never get satisfied with what you know and can do at any point in time. To make for progress, there is always something new to learn.

And if you are struggling in class, you do not need to throw in the towel or despair. What it just means is that you may either be doing the wrong thing or not doing the right thing correctly. What you need to do is to learn from your mistakes and change the way you think. Seek guidance to find your path. Once that is done, persist. And you will be amazed to find what you are capable of doing. Make maximum use of your elastic potential.

What you do today will either help secure your future or destroy it. Therefore, shun what will destroy it and follow after what will help secure it. And always remember that your future is the future of the country—good or bad.

GLOSSARY

Ablaze: in the process of burning; on fire

Abstract: a general idea or quality rather than an actual person, object, or event

Adventure: an exciting or dangerous experience

Amputate: to medically cut off (part of a person's body)

Analytical: related to using analysis or logical reasoning

Apex: the top or highest point of something

Arguably: as may be shown by argument

Arm: supply or provide with equipment, too, or other items in preparation or readiness for something

Artisan: someone who is skilled at making things by hand

Assign: to give someone a particular job or duty

Attribute: regard something as being caused by:

Autocracy: a form of government in which a country is ruled by a person or group with total power

Backdrop: the setting or conditions within which something happens

Bedrock: a strong idea, principle, or fact that supports something

Biographical: relating to or telling the story of a real person's life

Boomerang: an act or utterance that backfires on its originator

Brevity: the use of few words to say something

Cassock: a long gown worn by a priest

Catalyst: a person or event that quickly causes change or action

Chunk: a large amount or part of something

Circumstance: an event or fact that causes or helps something to happen,

Civility: polite, reasonable, and respectful behaviour

Competitive: related to or characterized by competition

Complement: something that completes something else or make it better

Complex: consisting of many different and connected parts

Complexity: the quality or state of not being simple; the quality of being complex

Composed: calm and in control of your emotions

Concept: an idea of what something is or how it works

Conducive: tending to promote or assist

Constrain: to limit or restrict (someone or something): to force someone to do something

Counterproductive: not helpful: tending to hinder the attainment of a desired goal

Cumbersome: hard to handle or manage because of size or weight: complicated and hard to do

Curious: having the desire to learn or know more about something or someone

Currency: a system of money in general use in a particular country

Daring: showing a lack of fear; willing to do dangerous or difficult things

Deflate: to release air or gas from something such as a tire or balloon

Delinquent: a young person who regularly does illegal or immoral things

Despair: the feeling of no longer having and hope

Deteriorate: to become worse as time passes

Detrimental: causing damage or injury

Dire: very bad: causing great fear or worry

Disguise: to change the usual appearance of something so that it will not be easily recognized

Disproportion: a difference that is not fair, reasonable or expected

Distant: existing or happening far away in space: far away in time

Divergent: differing from each other or from a standard

Duplicate: exactly the same as something else: made as an exact copy of something else

Endless: having or seeming to have no end or limit

Endowment: a person's natural ability or talent

Engender: to be the cause of source of (something)

Enhance: intensify, increase, or further improve the quality, value or extent of something

Entirety: the whole or total amount of something

Entrepreneur: a person who sets up a business or businesses

Erection: the state in which a body part (such as the penis) becomes firm and swollen because of sexual excitement

Escapade: an exciting, foolish, or dangerous experience or adventure

Eschew: to avoid (something) especially because you do not think it is right, proper, etc.

Essence: the basic nature of a thing; the quality or qualities that make a thing what it is

Euphemism: a mild or pleasant word or phrase that is used instead of one that is unpleasant or offensive

Expatriate: a person who lives in a foreign country

Expectancy: the state of thinking or hoping that something, especially something good will happen

Expedition: a journey or excursion undertaken for a specific purpose

Exploit: make full use of and derive benefit from something

Explore: travel through an unfamiliar area in other to learn about it

Extensive: having wide or considerable extent

Extravagance: the act or practice of spending a lot of money: wasteful or careless spending

Extrovert: an outgoing person

Facilitate: to make something easier or help cause something: to help something run more smoothly and effectively

Falsehood: an untrue statement

Fantasies: an act of imagining something

Fascinate: attract a strong attention or interest of someone

Fashionable: currently popular, or dressing and acting in a way that is currently popular

Fatal: causing death: causing ruin or failure

Feign: pretend

Fiction: stories about people and events that are not real

Flexibility: willing to change or try different things

Ford: to cross (an area of water) by walking or riding across a shallow part

Forecast: predict or estimate (a future event or trend)

Fundamental: an underlying ground, theory, or principle

Gad about: to go about without a specific aim or purpose

Genius: a very smart or talented person: a person who is very good at doing something

Genuine: actual, real, or true: not false or fake

Glamour: a very exciting and attractive quality

Grammatical: following the rules of grammar

Gravity: the natural force that tends to cause physical things to move towards each other

Habitual: done regularly or repeatedly

Hamper: to slow the movement or action, or progress of (someone or something)

Harness: to control and make use of a resource (a natural resource) especially to produce energy

Harvest: an accumulated store or productive result

Hazardous: involving risk or danger

Hesitate: to stop briefly before you do something especially because you are nervous or unsure about what to do

Ignorance: **lack** of knowledge, understanding, or education: the state of being ignorant

Illustrate: to give examples in order to make (something) easier to understand

Impaired: diminished in function or ability

Impediment: a hindrance or obstruction in doing something

Impose: force an unwelcome decision or ruling on someone

Impression: an idea, feeling or opinion about something or someone, especially one formed on the basis of little experience

Indifferent: not interested in or concern about something

Inferior: a little or less importance or value

Inquiry: the act of asking questions in order to collect or gather information

Interpret: to explain the meaning of something

Interrupt: to cause (something) to stop happening for a time

Invalid: suffering from a disease or disability

Invariably: always

Invention: the action of inventing something, typically a device or process

Investigate: carry out a systematic or formal inquiry to discover and examine the fact (an incident, allegation, etc.) so as to establish the truth

Irreparable: too bad to be corrected or repaired

Irrespective of: without thinking about or considering (something)

Isolation: the state of being in a place or situation that is separate from others

Manoeuvre: a clever or skilful action or movement

Manipulate: to use or change (numbers, information, etc.) in a skilful way or for a particular purpose

Marvel: one that causes wonder or astonishment

Master: to learn (something) completely: to get the knowledge and skill that allows you to do, use, or understand (something) very well

Medicinal: a substance or plant that has healing properties

Microsecond: one millionth of a second: a very short period of time

Misconception: a view or opinion that is incorrect because it is based on faulty thinking or understanding

Mis-educate: badly or wrongly educate

Monarchy: a form of government in which a country is ruled by a monarch (such as a king or queen)

Monstrous: very ugly, cruel or vicious

Museum: a building in which interesting and valuable things such as paintings and sculptures or scientific or historical objects) are collected and shown to the public

Mutual: shared by two or more people or groups

Obeisance: a movement of your body (such as bowing) that shows respect for someone or something

Obnoxious: unpleasant in a way that makes people feel offended, annoyed, or disgusted

Optimal: best or most effective

Overhauling: changing something completely in order to improve it

Overwhelming: used to describe something that is so confusing, difficult, etc., that you feel unable to do it

Painstaking: diligent care and effort

Pamper: to treat with extreme or excessive care and attention

Pang: a sudden, strong feeling of physical or emotional pain

Paramount: of the highest rank of importance

Passionate: having, showing or caused by strong feelings or belief

Pathway: a line of communication over interconnecting neurons extending from one organ or centre to another

Perspective: the interrelation in which a subject or its parts are mentally viewed

Persuade: to cause (someone) to do something by asking, arguing, or giving reasons

Pervasive: existing in every part of something or spreading to all parts of something

Photographic: capable of retaining vivid impressions

Placard: a large notice or sign put up in a public place or carried by people

Platter: a large plate that is used for serving food and especially meat

Plump: having a full rounded shape: slightly fat

Ponder: think about or consider (something) carefully

Potential: a quality something has that can be developed to make it better

Precious: very valuable or important

Priceless: extremely valuable or important

Principal: most important

Productivity: the state or quality of being productive

Proficient: good at doing something

Promising: full of promise: likely to succeed or to yield good results

Prostrate: lying with the front of your body turned toward the ground

Pursue: follow or chase something or someone: to try to get or do (something) over a period of time

Quest: A long or hard search for something

Ravage: damage or harm very badly

Reckless: not showing proper concern about the possible bad results of your actions

Recur: occur again periodically or repeatedly

Reference: the act of mentioning something in speech or writing

Relate: to show or make a connection between

Religiously: very careful to do something whenever it can or should be done

Remarkable: unusual or surprising: likely to be noticed

Replete: filled with something

Reputation: the common opinion that people have about someone or something

Requisite: needed for a particular purpose

Resolve: to make a definite and serious decision to do something

Rife: very common

Sacrilege: the treatment of something sacred or highly valued with great disrespect

Scoundrel: a person who is cruel or dishonest

Servile: very obedient and trying so hard to please someone

Shun: to avoid (someone or something)

Significant: very important

Spectator: a person who watches an event, show, game, or activity, etc., often as part of an audience

Spectrum: a continuous sequence or range

Squalid: very dirty and unpleasant; immoral or dishonest

Square: an open place or area formed at the meeting of two or more streets

Startling: very surprising, shocking, or frightening

Steer clear of: to avoid

Substitute: a person or thing that takes the place of someone or something else

Symbiosis: the relationship between two different kinds of living things that live together and depend on one other

Term: a word or phrase used to describe a thing or to express an idea

Underestimate: to think of (someone or something) as being lower in ability, influence, or value than that person or thing actually is

Unhealthy: risky or unsound

Unique: used to say that someone or something is unlike anyone or something else

Unthinkable: impossible to imagine or believe: too bad or shocking to be thought of

Upshot: the final result, or outcome

Venture: a new activity, project or business, etc., that typically involves risk

Vice versa: used to say that the opposite of something is true

Virtually: very nearly; almost entirely

Well-rounded: educated in many different subjects: fully or broadly developed

BIBLIOGRAPHY

Beghetto, A. R. & Kaufman, C. J. (2010): *Nurturing Creativity In The Classroom*. New York, Cambridge University Press.

Blackaby, H. Blackaby R. (2011): *Spiritual Leadership*. Nashville, Tennessee, B&H Publishing Group.

Bruess, C. & Greenberg S. J. (1994): *Sexuality Education, Theory and Practice*. 3rd Ed. USA, Wm. C. Brown Communications, Inc.

Erickson, H. L. (2008): *Stirring the Head, Heart and Soul*. 3rd Ed. London, UK, SAGE Ltd.

Feldman, R. S. (2003): *Power Learning*. 2nd Ed. New York, McGraw-Hill https://en.m.wikipedia.org 04-03-21

https://www.farnamstreetblog.com 04-03-21

Kayport, N. (2014): *Social and Cultural Anthropology*. 3rd Ed. New York, Routledge.

Krusen, C. (2016): *They were Christians, The inspiring faith of men and women who changed the world*. USA, Baker Books.

Maxwell, J. C. (2014): *How Successful People Grow*. California, Center Street.

Morrish, M. (1983): *Development In The Third World*. Oxford, Oxford Printing Press.

Santrock, J. W. (2004): *Adolescence*. 5th Ed. New York, McGraw-Hill.

Steiner, C. (2003): *Emotional Literacy, Intelligence with a Heart*. California, USA, Personhood Press.

Strauss, M. G. (2018): *The Creator Revealed*. IN, USA, WestBow Press.

White, R. W. (1976): *The Enterprise of Living, A View of Personal Growth*. 2nd Ed. USA, Holt, Rinehart Winston, Inc.

Witter, M. (2013): *Reading Without Limits*. CA, USA, Jossey-Bass.

www.ingramcontent.com/pod-product-compliance
Ingram Content Group UK Ltd.
Pitfield, Milton Keynes, MK11 3LW, UK
UKHW022210230426
12048UKWH00016BA/754